Musings
through Mark

a story devotional
through the Gospel of Mark

Sarah Woodall

md
PUBLISHING

20 19 18 17 16 15   7 6 5 4 3 2 1

First published by Malcom Down Publishing 2015.
www.malcolmdown.co.uk

British Library Cataloguing in Publication Data

A catalogue record for this book is available from the British Library

ISBN 978-1-910786-29-1

Printed in the UK
Cover design by Tim Pettingale

Dedication

For Mum, Dad and Owain.
Thank you for believing in me
through all the years.

And for Mabel and Evan –
who loved us as their own.
xxx

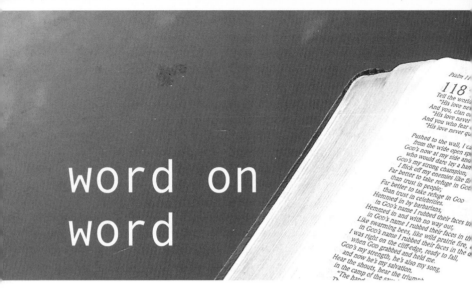

word on word

I began writing this story devotional in a red notebook.

The cover had that rich earth, mingled with mahogany depth, kind of feel. It was inviting. And there was a desire within me for a fresh encounter with Jesus. To see Him deeper. To know Him deeper.

And so I began a journey.

In early morning scribbles, I came as honestly as I could to the Gospel of Mark, the first written account of Jesus' life. Armed only with coffee cup and a seeking heart, my musings began to be played out on the keys of an old typewriter. The clack of keys filled the cool attic room with the clamour of my oh-so-frail attempts to set down mystery. In the pressing out of each thought, ink met with blank page, and I met with The Author.

The One who is always seeking us…
…That we might really know Him.

Taking photographs became part of my journey. The images were a learner's attempt to express, with fresh sight, something of the story.

And so the words (which turned into my **tallpapertrees.wordpress.com** blog) and the pictures (often taken on my phone and then on my first 'proper' camera) became this which you now hold: *Musings Through Mark.*

This story devotion travels all the way through the Gospel, and is best enjoyed with a coffee cup in hand and a little time to linger. It is filled with narrative, with poetic thought, with play, with story, and with a good sprinkle of imagination.

These musings are not a theological masterpiece. No, each one is simply a stumbling response to Redemption's Story.

Each one is a desire, and an invitation, to see.

I pray as you journey with me, that you may see more of Jesus. That you may fall more in love with him, and that you may discover more of your own place within His great story.

Sarah xxx

And so the story begins, word on word…

day 1
the
beginning

"Look, I am sending my messenger ahead of you, and he will prepare your way. He is a voice shouting in the wilderness, 'Prepare the way for the Lord's coming!' ...This messenger was John the Baptist ... John announced: 'Someone is coming soon who is greater than I am—so much greater…'"
[Mark 1v1-7 NLT]

And so the book is opened and the story begins.

With each turn of page, life is created in colours bright and bold, breathing the world anew. With each turn of phrase, love-filled lines unfurl and unfold, scribing the years in grace and truth.

For this is redemption's tale, reaching ever forwards and ever back …
Way back, before trust was torn.
Way back, before lives were dashed upon the brokenness of us all.
Way back, before the beginning of the beginning

To The Author.

Who wrote His story with love so deep,
Love so wide, love so true,
Engraving upon all the years,
The promise of
One to come.

One to lift the earthen from the dust,
One to mend the tare of hearts so torn,
One to breath us warm to life

In the begin again of
New Creation.

And now, the time had come…

So who is Jesus?

Jesus is the beginning.

Something to consider

The message of Jesus didn't originate in a backstreet barn of Bethlehem. It wasn't conceived in the mind of Mark the man, or the prophets of old. It wasn't a new idea, for it began way back in the heart of God who had promised His deliverer.

And now, with all the expectation of the centuries filling his lungs, John the messenger proclaims Jesus the promised One.

And in this One, we can find a new beginning.

Maybe we can welcome Jesus to do a new thing in us, to bring his new creation into our hearts and lives. For He whispers into every part of our story the chance for heaven's Begin Again.

Something to pray

My Jesus, thank you that you can create everything new. Please breathe your life into the dusty places of my heart, please make all things new in me. Thank you that you are the promised One. Thank you that you bring the Begin Again of new creation. Amen.

water to the thirsty

"Thunder in the desert! Prepare for God's arrival! ... John the Baptizer appeared in the wild, preaching a baptism of life-change that leads to forgiveness of sins ... As he preached he said, 'The real action comes next: The star in this drama, to whom I'm a mere stagehand, will change your life. I'm baptizing you here in the river, turning your old life in for a kingdom life. His baptism—a holy baptism by the Holy Spirit—will change you from the inside out.'"
[Mark 1v3-8 The Message]

The messenger begins to prepare the way, his words rumbling through arid hearts, like…

Thunder in the desert,
And everything unsettles in the sound.
Thunder in the desert,
Announcing a turning back, a turning towards, a turnaround.
Thunder in the desert,
Spurring the parched to seek the source where water can be found.

For soon heaven's floodgates would be opened wide,
Soon cascades of grace would be raining down.

Drenching the earth trodden out of drought, in the downpour.
Quenching the soul parched out of desiccation, in the outpour
Of all that was to come. Of He who was to come…

He who is water to the thirsty.

He who turns every desert, into grace soaked ground.

So who is Jesus?

Jesus is water to the thirsty.

Something to consider

John the messenger prepared the way for Jesus: The promised One, the Holy One, the One who clothed himself with the dust of our humanity and walked among us.

Considering who Jesus is, you would expect that it would be us bringing Him a gift. Us giving, Him receiving.
But Jesus came bringing the gift to us. The gift of Himself, the gift of His life, the gift of His Spirit.

This gift is not just a baptism of water, easily trickling away, but it is the gift of submerging. Where His life wells up on the inside of us, turning all the desert places into grace soaked ground.

Are there any areas of life where stagnation has set in? Where there is a dryness of the soul? Maybe we can ask Jesus to bring his life and Spirit into every space of our hearts. For He is water to the thirsty.

Something to pray

My Jesus, thank you that you want to fill me with your Holy Spirit, your living water. Please fill me full with you. Please come into all the stagnant places of my heart, so I may be submerged in your life and grace. Thank you that you are water to my thirsty soul. Amen.

the way maker

"At this time, Jesus came from Nazareth in Galilee and was baptized by John in the Jordan. The moment he came out of the water, he saw the sky split open and God's Spirit, looking like a dove, come down on him. Along with the Spirit, a voice: 'You are my Son, chosen and marked by my love, pride of my life.'"
[Mark 1v9-11 The Message]

The story was unfolding…
And onto the bustling riverside scene, walks a man with carpentry-calloused hands. Just one with a lilt thicker than the city-edged tongue. Just one in the jostling crowd.
Not many turn their heads,
For quiet he comes, cloaked in years of obscurity.

Yet, heaven is tiptoe watching.
To see when dusty feet slice waters blue, when calloused hands submerge in trust running deep, when the eternal ushers in on grace-filled wings.

For this one,
Is the One worthy,
The One loved,
The One holy.

Stepping deep into surrender,
Becoming the Way Maker,
So calloused hearts, can be washed clean.

So who is Jesus?

Jesus is the way maker.

Something to consider

Jesus did not need to be baptised, he did not have the marks of the fallen on Him, there was nothing in Him that required a washing away. He was right with God. And yet His baptism reveals heart surrender and paints deliverance deeper onto the picture. Pointing to how God would forge the way through Him for us to walk into new life, so that our calloused hearts could be forever washed clean.

Before He did anything that made Him noticeable on earth, Jesus trusted His way to the Father who loved Him.

And it makes me wonder if there areas of my heart where there is striving to make my own way? Maybe instead I could trust my way to Jesus, the one who is the Way Maker.

Something to pray

My Jesus, thank you that you came to make the way so my calloused heart, can be washed clean. I surrender my way to you. I let go of all my striving, and simply trust you to be the one who is the Way Maker. Amen.

day 4

shattered
spaces

"The Spirit then compelled Jesus to go into the wilderness, where he was tempted by Satan for forty days. He was out among the wild animals, and angels took care of him. Later on, after John was arrested, Jesus went into Galilee, where he preached God's Good News. 'The time promised by God has come at last!' he announced. 'The Kingdom of God is near! Repent of your sins and believe the Good News!'"
[Mark 1v12-15 NLT]

The carpenter man began to walk where the wild things are.

Through the heart-fractured lands where the ground beneath is unrelenting. Where jagged rocks of lack cut deep, sharp slithers of longing stab hard, and broken living threatens to destroy.

These are the terrains of tested trust.
These are the shattered spaces.
These are the wilderness places.

He did not run from such as these.

And there was evening, and there was morning,
And still He stood
In solid rock trust.

And there was evening, and there was morning,
And still He knew

His God would be enough.

So who is Jesus?

Jesus is enough.

Something to consider

Jesus took the path through the wilderness. Reverberating the reminder of a desert road taken long ago, where into a forty-year landscape of need and trial, God was enough.

He gave His people water from the rock when they were thirsty. He gave food from heaven when they were hungry. He was the pillar of strength for them in their night. He was the cloud of guidance for them in their day.

And onto the rocks of their wilderness, He etched out the promise of Himself.

And there was evening, and He would be their God. And there was morning, and He would bring them through. And for all their evenings and all their mornings, He would be enough.

In the wilderness Jesus stood in solid trust, declaring that God was enough. When He came out of the wilderness, He proclaimed the same.

For all our evenings, and for all our mornings, will we trust that He will be enough?

Something to pray

My Jesus, thank you that you walked though the wilderness places and stood on solid rock trust. Into all the shattered spaces of my life, please help me know that there is grace enough, love enough, and strength enough from you. Thank you that for all my evenings, and all my mornings, you will always be enough. Amen.

day 5
salt of
the sea

"One day as Jesus was walking along the shore of the Sea of Galilee, he saw Simon and his brother Andrew throwing a net into the water, for they fished for a living. Jesus called out to them, "Come, follow me, and I will show you how to fish for people!" And they left their nets at once and followed him … "
[Mark 1v16-20 NLT]

Getting up before the glint of dawn, treading well-worn paths, heading to the waters edge of familiar, of hard work, of the creak of boats through storm and calm, of the creak of hearts through the way it had always been.

These were the salt of the sea type ones.

Ones living in the ebb and flow of days washing in, and days washing out. Ones living to the tides and patterns of mending nets, spreading nets, gathering nets. Ones knotted right through with the ordinary.

Did the God who painted dawn each day, notice them? Did the God who carved out clouds from sky, see them? Did the God of the way back, and of the way forward, want them?

They hoped He did.

And then along the paths of their familiar, walks the carpenter man.

He notices them. He sees them. He calls them.

And these salt of the sea type ones marvel as dawn is painted into their ordinary.

The dawn of God's Kingdom come.

So who is Jesus?

Jesus is the One who sees.

Something to consider

The invitation of God reached these ordinary fisherlads. And in Jesus' call and their follow, the 'ordinary' became an ocean of possibility.

They became ones living in the ebb and flow of grace washing in and mercy washing out. Ones knotted right through with the new ordinary, which is anything but ordinary, of God's Kingdom come.

Please know that in the midst of your ordinary, God notices you. He sees you. Maybe today you could invite Him to create a new ordinary in you, an ordinary filled right through with oceans of His possibility.

Something to pray

My Jesus, thank you that you see me. You notice every detail of my life and you love me. I want to walk with you, to see what you see, and to follow where you call. Please come into the ordinary of my life and fill it with you. Please fill my days and years with all the possibility of your Kingdom come. Amen.

day 6
open window

"Jesus lost no time in getting to the meeting place. He spent the day there teaching. They were surprised at his teaching – so forthright, so confident – not quibbling and quoting like the religion scholars.
Suddenly, while still in the meeting place, he was interrupted by a man who was deeply disturbed and yelling out 'What business do you have here with us, Jesus? Nazarene! I know what you're up to! You're the Holy One of God, and you've come to destroy us!' Jesus shut him up: 'Quiet! Get out of him!' The afflicting spirit … got out … " [Mark 1v21-28 The Message]

A meeting place stuffed with empty words. Where the air to breathe is stifled in the shout of the show. Where the strive has strangled the life out of living.

Here the people gather. Some with a gasp of hope. Some without.

And into the suffocation comes the carpenter man. Unsettling the air of stagnation. Opening the window wide. The Message, tells of The message. The Promised One, talks of The promise. The Holy One, utters The holy.

Every molecule of space tingles with His words. Words weighted with fullness. Words weightless like spirit, like breath, like a gust of air in a stagnant room.

Wind Words, breathing life again. Silencing oppression's claim, shaking the matter of dark chaos, conceiving new creation.

And the bound one becomes a windswept one, as he inhales deep lungfuls of freedom.

The window is opened wide, and all can breathe again.

So who is Jesus?

Jesus is the bringer of the Wind Words.

Something to consider

Sometimes we get so used to our situations being the way they are, that we stop hoping things can change. We stop gasping for breath, we stop longing for God's air in our lungs, or having expectation in His words. At other times we don't realise that life has become full of striving, and that we need to be windswept once again.

Are there any areas of life where it's time to welcome God's Wind Words afresh?

Something to pray

Thank you Jesus that your words are weighted with fullness, and weightless like freedom. Thank you that I can trust your words. Jesus, please breathe your Wind Words into my heart, please fill me with your Spirit. I want to be windswept in you again. Amen.

day 7

hope
kindled

"After Jesus left the synagogue with James and John, they went to Simon and Andrew's home. Now Simon's mother-in-law was sick in bed with a high fever. They told Jesus about her right away. So he went to her bedside, took her by the hand, and helped her sit up. Then the fever left her ... That evening after sunset, many sick and demon-possessed people were brought to Jesus. The whole town gathered at the door to watch. So Jesus healed many…"
[Mark 1v 29-34 NLT]

Fire hearted and warmed right through, they headed home. Awe flickering across their horizon with a story unfolding. A story as old as time. A story as young as day.

Heaven was painting earth aflame and they blinked and beheld. Wide-eyed.

After all the years of waiting, after all the embers nearly dying, hope was kindling. Before, there was not a lot to be done about fever burning through a body. Not a lot to be done about any of it. But now…

…They watched as he took her by the hand. The heat of fever had to give way, as the white-hot brush strokes of kingdom come redefined her horizon. It was sundown. Red and orange spread across the sky, and 'Hope kindled' spread across the whole town.

They gathered at the door and watched as heaven painted earth aflame.

So who is Jesus?

Jesus is the hope kindler.

Something to consider

With Jesus, hope can come into any situation, no matter how desperate it is. He is the bringer of heaven to earth. Maybe there are things that we are facing, where we need Jesus to step in. Maybe we can invite Jesus to kindle hope within us, and to redefine life's horizons once again.

Something to pray

My Jesus, thank you that with you, all things are possible. You can bring life and hope for me, and for those around me. Thank you that you want to redefine my horizons, and paint life aflame. Where the embers of faith feel fragile, please kindle hope in my heart. Please unfold your story in me. Amen.

day 8
breathe easy

"While it was still night, way before dawn, he got up and went out to a secluded spot and prayed. Simon and those with him went looking for him. They found him and said "Everybody's looking for you." Jesus said, "Let's go to the rest of the villages so I can preach there also. This is why I have come." [Mark 1v35-39 The Message]

The earth, stillness cloaked. The air, silence woven. The night, blanket-like as the un-definition of darkness wraps itself around.

All is still. And the earth waits.

All is still. And the once upon a (must have seemed a long ago) time carpenter waits.

Ears open, eyes open, spirit open. Breathing in, breathing out.

After the noise of the night before. After the success and the frenzy. After the awe-struck commotion.

He waits. And the earth holds its breath, not wishing to disturb.

So all is still, and still He waits for the sacred space of heart encounter. Ears open, eyes open. Seeking out the place of meeting.

Breathing in, breathing deep the prayer uttered in seclusion. Until He is clothed in the dawn of defining light.

And when the quiet is shattered by the want, the need, the demand... He breathes easy. For His heart is woven with the cause and the call. His life is threaded in the Father.

And the clamour is stilled, in the breathing in and breathing out of heart encounter.

So who is Jesus?

Jesus is the one who breathes easy.

Something to consider

Jesus did not treat the open access He had to the Father, lightly. He was the seeker of the Father. Jesus, the Son of God, the one who was completely loved by God, the one who Himself was God, longed for alone time with God. He desired it, He needed it. And out of that secret place of intimacy, Jesus walked in clarity and direction. He lived and breathed out of heart encounter.

The question is, do we?

Do we, the loved of God, the ones who now also have open access to God, do we seek heart time with God? For, His heart is always seeking us.

Maybe it's time to find the place of heart encounter once again.

Something to pray

My Jesus, I love you and I am so glad I am yours, but sometimes I am distracted by all the stuff of life. Please draw close to me as my heart is seeking you. Please help me breathe easy in you. Amen.

day 9

the story maker

"A man with leprosy came and knelt in front of Jesus begging to be healed. 'If you are willing, you can heal me and make me clean,' he said.
Moved with compassion, Jesus reached out and touched him. 'I am willing,' he said. 'Be healed!' Instantly the leprosy disappeared, and the man was healed."
[Mark 1v40–41 NLT]

Word was spreading fast. Stories were reaching across landscapes, stories were crossing borders. Stories dancing on the tongues of the once mute, stories glimmering in the eyes of the once blind. Stories stretching to the out of town type places, the out of favour, outcast and ousted-out type spaces.

The man had watched dignity rot with his decaying flesh. He had watched life pass (and too many lives pass) into numbness.

And then the stories came. Stories hitting hard, like a punch in the gut. Right where it hurts. Right into the pit of pain. Winding him out of numbness so that he felt it full force.

He wasn't meant to leave the out-of-favour space he occupied. But he had to.

So he pushed his way through and fell at the feet of the Story Maker.

The man, broken in every way. The Story Maker, willing in every way.

And with a word, life was rewritten.

And with an outstretched hand, the ousted-out was welcomed in.

So who is Jesus?

Jesus is the Story Maker.

Something to consider

Sometimes we hear amazing stories of what God does in other people's lives, and it reminds us of the pain in our own. We can think that a 'good story' is just for them.

However this man's life speaks of something different. It speaks of our God who is not only able, but who is willing. Our God is willing, even for those of us who sometimes feel out of favour, or outcast.

God wants to write a different story into our lives. He wants to write a good story.

Something to pray

My Jesus, thank you that you are moved with compassion when I go through the hard things of life. Thank you that you are able and you are willing. Thank you that you are good, and you are for me. Thank you that through what you did on the cross, I am forever in your favour. My hope is you. Please come and write your good story into my life. Amen.

day 10

to the heart
of the matter

"…four men arrived carrying a paralyzed man on a mat. They
couldn't bring him to Jesus because of the crowd, so they dug
a hole through the roof above his head. Then they lowered the
man … Seeing their faith, Jesus said to the paralyzed man,
'My child, your sins are forgiven.'
But some of the teachers of religious law who were sitting
there thought to themselves, '…Only God can forgive sins!'
… Then Jesus turned to the paralyzed man and said, 'Stand
up, pick up your mat, and go home!' And the man jumped up,
grabbed his mat, and walked… "
[Mark 2v1-12 NLT]

Resignation had set like blood thickened, and the man was set in the standstill. The lie still and let it all fade. His life, like joints stiffened with congealed years. The dream, like substance becoming shadow.

And yet, they would not give in. They had to get to Him.

Ahead was a barred way of shoulder-to-shoulder obstruction but with flinted faces, they scrambled. With every fistful of roof removed something was shifting, something was forged within. Until they emerged, bold as brass.

Others looked on with indignation, but He saw right to the heart. This once upon a carpenter was skilled at mending the broken things. His words like oil upon the rust-tight places. His grace, unlocking everything.

And so shadow took on substance, joints took on movement, and the paralysed one grabbed his mat and walked. Treading on forgiven steps. Flint faced in freedom. Bold as brass.

So who is Jesus?

Jesus is the key.

Something to consider

Jesus speaks right to the heart of the matter. Whether we recognise ourselves in the man on the mat, needing to hear words of grace-filled forgiveness. Or whether we find ourselves in the ones tearing off the roof. The cry about a dream, a promise, a longing, calling us to have bold as brass faith. Wherever we find ourselves in this story, Jesus is the key. He opens the way.

Something to pray

My Jesus, thank you that you do the impossible things. You make the way for my heart to be forgiven and made whole. You cause impassable obstructions to be transformed into open doors. I come to you in bold faith, knowing that you are the one who puts substance onto the shadow of my dreams. You are the one who restores and heals. You are relentless in your love and powerful in how you act. Amen.

day 11
the
invitation

"…he saw Levi, son of Alpaeus, at his work collecting taxes. Jesus said, 'Come along with me.'
…The religion scholars and Pharisees saw him keeping this kind of company and lit into his disciples: 'What kind of example is this, acting cosy with the riffraff?'
Jesus, overhearing, shot back, 'Who needs a doctor: the healthy or the sick? I'm here inviting the sin-sick, not the spiritually-fit.'"
[Mark 2v13-17 The Message]

The people were peckish, and He once again spread a feast.

Morsels of wisdom. The taste of grace. Food for the starving.

The religious ones stood on the edge looking full. Unaware of the famine within.

Panning through the crowds, He spotted one.

One of the unlikely. One of the hungry. One of the least.

And then came the invitation.

Shaking all norms and sending shock waves right though. The fisherlads were getting used to this by now. The religious never could.

The man looked up, as surprised as the rest.

All eyes were on him, judging him by what they saw. He had gorged on greed and was famished within. He knew he was undeserving, but oh, how he longed for a taste of grace.

Then with a smile, the once upon a carpenter called out to him.

And the Lord of heaven and earth pulled up a chair, welcoming the unlikely to the feast.

So who is Jesus?

Jesus is the invitation.

Something to consider

Jesus welcomes who-so-ever would come, to the feast of His goodness. To come close, and to know His friendship. To taste and see the love of the Father. To have Life now, and forevermore. It is a gift of surprising and undeserved grace.

But how often do we discount ourselves from partaking in this goodness, when Jesus is always pulling up a chair for us, and inviting us in.

Something to pray

My Jesus, thank you that you have made room for me, and you want me to be close to you. Thank you that your invitation remains constant, whatever my life has looked like. You are worth following with my everything. And so with deep gratitude, I say yes please to all you are, and all you have prepared for me. I gladly come to your feast. Amen.

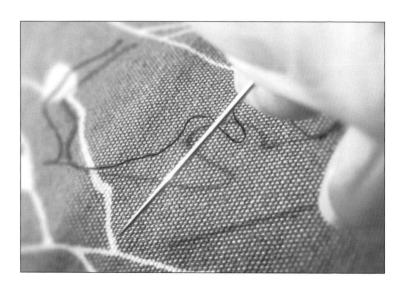

day 12
stitch on
stitch

"Besides, who would patch old clothing with new cloth?
For the new patch would shrink and rip away from the old
cloth, leaving an even bigger tear than before.
And no one puts new wine into old wineskins. For the
wine would burst the wineskins, and the wine and the
skins would both be lost.
New wine calls for new wineskins."
[Mark 2v18-22 NLT]

The old pattern wouldn't fit anymore.

Seasons were in the shift of old giving way to new,

Of making room,

Of life bursting through every tired seam.

Some tried to cling to the ragged wisps of the strive, those strands offering only a scrap of tattered dignity. But this was something brand new. No ragtag repair.

This was new cloth, to cover the nakedness of human shame.

New cloth, woven in blood red.

New cloth, embroidered through with threaded love,

Lacing us into redemption's gown

Stitch on stitch on stitch.

And it was time to celebrate. So He led the way in the delight of all things new. The Master Tailor in his Father's grand design.

So who is Jesus?

Jesus is the Master Tailor.

Something to consider

Sometimes we try to cling to the old. The old pattern of how things work. The old pattern of how things didn't work. The old striving of us trying to make our way to God, and trying to make our way in the world.

But Jesus makes a new way. He clothes us in his rightness with God. He weaves redemption into our story, and threads us into His story. He is the Master Tailor who loves creating something new, even today.

Something to pray

My Jesus, thank you that you are the Master Tailor. Thank you that you have made the way for me to be clothed in right standing before the Father.

Thank you that you love doing a new thing, and even today are working beauty and redemption into my story. I trust your design and welcome the new things you want to do in and through me. Amen.

a sea of gold

"One Sabbath day as Jesus was walking through some grain fields, his disciples began breaking off heads of grain to eat. But the Pharisees said to Jesus, 'Look, why are they breaking the law by harvesting grain on the Sabbath?' … Then Jesus said to them, 'The Sabbath was made to meet the needs of people, and not people to meet the requirements of the Sabbath. So the Son of Man is Lord, even over the Sabbath!'"
[Mark 2v23-28 NLT]

Wading through a sea of gold, as curls of corn circled. Ears prickled with the rustle of warmed stalk and stem. Tongues tingled in the crunch of amber seed. And they walked through earth's garden.

Man with their Maker.

Did thoughts stretch back to long-gone skies, when new plants reached for the fresh sun of earth awakened, when peace of heart was given?

Now, like then, accusation disturbed the ripening seed,
But the Windswept One silenced their black and white distortion.

Their ears bristled with the sound of freedom, as the Lord of the Sabbath redefined the law in coloured Gold.

And in a saffron sea, those born of dust, once again walked free.

Man with their Maker.

So who is Jesus?

Jesus is the one who brings freedom.

Something to consider

Sometimes we listen to accusation. Those warped things about who God is, and about who we are. Those accusations which try to steal the moments, and try to hinder our life with God. However, God's word brings liberty.

God's plan is always about us walking close with Him, just like at the beginning. So, may we let His words redefine our lives in peace, in truth, and in freedom.

Something to pray

My Jesus, you have dealt with everything that separates me from you. Thank you that at the cross you silenced every accusation against me, enabling me to walk close with you. Please come and redefine my life with your words. Please help me walk in your freedom. Amen.

day 14
found in the
re-form

"Jesus went into the synagogue again and noticed a man with a deformed hand. Since it was the Sabbath, Jesus' enemies watched him closely … Jesus said … 'Does the law permit good deeds on the Sabbath, or is it a day for doing evil? … ' He looked around at them angrily and was deeply saddened by their hard hearts. Then he said to the man, 'Hold out your hand.' So the man held out his hand, and it was restored!"
[Mark 3v1-6 NLT]

Hard ridged. Unyielding in granite resolve. Gnarled through the years and now fixed in the jagged formation of twist and bend and warp and bow.

They were buckled in the distort.

It was the deformation of heart and His molten anger boiled at the craggy landscape of their misconceptions.

For they did not see the man, they did not know the love of the Father.

But the once upon a carpenter did.

And so he began the re-form.

Straightening the man's hand and confronting their twisted centre.

Redefining, rearranging, restoring, realigning.

Opening wide the cavernous depths of mercy.

Inviting each one to be

Found in the re-form.

So who is Jesus?

Jesus is the re-form.

Something to consider

Sometimes we have a very distorted view of God. We see Him like the Pharisees did, as one yielding harsh judgement, just waiting to see us fall. Jesus was saddened by their misunderstanding and angered by their misrepresentation of God. Their heart deformation robbed them, and others, from truly knowing the Father.

God is so holy that we cannot even begin to fathom it, but His heart is also shaped in mercy and love. That is what the cross was all about.

Maybe take a little time and ask Jesus to help you see any misconceptions you have about the love of God. And let Jesus bring the re-form into the depths of your heart.

Something to pray

My Jesus, thank you that you came to reveal the heart of the Father. His heart shaped in mercy and compassion, as well as in holiness. Please show me any areas where my understanding of you is twisted and warped. Please be the re-form in my life, so that more and more I may know you as you really are. Amen.

day 15
holding
steady

"A huge crowd from Galilee trailed after them … He had healed many people, and now everyone who had something wrong was pushing and shoving to get near and touch him. Evil spirits, when they recognized him, fell down and cried out, 'You are the Son of God!' But Jesus would have none of it. He shut them up, forbidding them to identify him in public."
[Mark 3v7-12 The Message]

A horde of demand swarmed over the landscape, teeming with the swell and surge of insistent claim. Trying to force their way.

Pressing hard.
Pressing close.
Pressing in.

But the once upon a carpenter, held steady.

Into the frenzy of desperation came the scream of evil, shrieking in provocation. Feeding off the din and commotion and intent on inciting poisoned schemes.
Trying to force His hand.

Pressing hard.
Pressing close.
Pressing in.

But He would not play their septic game. And in the push and the shove, in the crush and the trample, in the scream and clamour…

The once upon a carpenter, held steady.

So who is Jesus?

Jesus is our steadfast.

Something to consider

Jesus wasn't driven by striving to be recognised, or by the need for vindication. He would not allow things to be pushed before the proper time and did not bow to evil's schemes. He was living according to God's approval and to God's plan. And in that, He could hold steady, even when facing great pressure.

With Jesus in us, we can hold steady too.

Whether we are facing pressure within, or pressure without, know that Jesus is our steadfast. As we cling to Him, He will enable us to hold steady.

Something to pray

My Jesus, thank you that you are my steadfast. You are the unwavering, unfaltering one who loves me with loyal love, and who is with me in committed strength. Please help me hold steady in you, whatever the pressures I am facing. I cling to you as my steadfast. Amen.

day
16
forever
named

"He climbed a mountain and invited those he wanted with
him. They climbed together. He settled on twelve, and
designated them apostles. The plan was that they would
be with him, and he would send them out to proclaim the
Word and give them authority to banish demons. These are
the twelve: Simon (Jesus later named him Peter, meaning
"Rock"), James, son of Zebedee, John, brother of James (Jesus
nicknamed the Zebedee brothers Boanerges, meaning "Sons
of Thunder"), Andrew, Philip, Bartholomew, Matthew, Thomas,
James, son of Alphaeus, Thaddaeus, Simon the Canaanite,
Judas Iscariot (who betrayed him)."
[Mark 3v13-19 The Message]

Further up, away from the noise, He welcomed them into the ascent.

The meaning of the mountain was written in the chronicles of their history, carved in the geography of their identity.

The mountain place. Where God met with his people.

Hallowed ground. Holy terrain.

Yet further up, away from the noise He welcomed them.

These undignified ones. Unqualified for anything other than net and scale and hook and line. Hands rough with lowly years and hearts shaped in anonymity's tide.

In the mountain place, now named.

Now written into the chronicles of history, with the commission forever carved in the geography of their identity.

They had been Named, to bear His Name.

So who is Jesus?

Jesus is the one who Names us.

Something to consider

The disciples never would have thought that they were worthy. And the truth is, they weren't. For the truth is, none of us are.

And yet He chose them, He wanted them, He called them to walk with Him, the One who is Holy.

And we, like them, are unworthy.
And we like them, are called by name.

You are named to bear His name…

Something to pray

My Jesus, thank you that you call me by my name. Thank you that you welcome me to stand on holy ground and be close to you. I am one of the unworthy, and also one of the forever grateful, that you have called me to come. You have named me to bear your name. Amen.

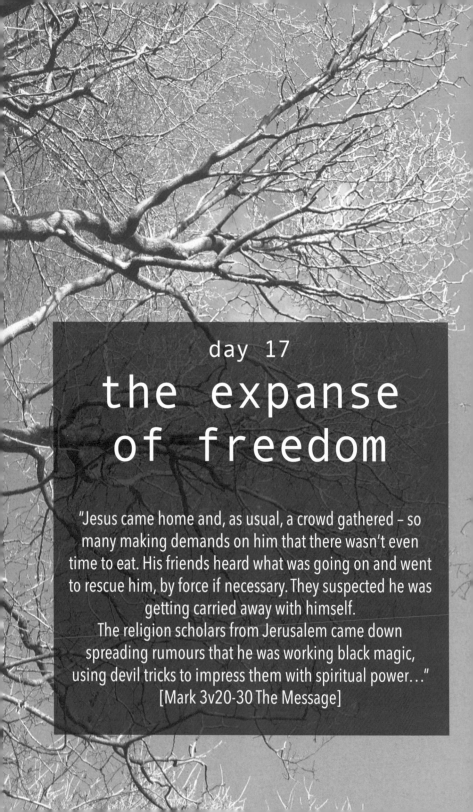

day 17

the expanse
of freedom

"Jesus came home and, as usual, a crowd gathered – so
many making demands on him that there wasn't even
time to eat. His friends heard what was going on and went
to rescue him, by force if necessary. They suspected he was
getting carried away with himself.
The religion scholars from Jerusalem came down
spreading rumours that he was working black magic,
using devil tricks to impress them with spiritual power…"
[Mark 3v20-30 The Message]

It didn't fit with how they thought it should go.

It didn't shrink small and sit comfortably contained into box tight thinking.

This expanse of freedom.

But they couldn't see it, or wouldn't see it,

Still he tried to show them the sky.

This wide span of grace stretching across the heavens. This vastness of liberty, broadening with every breath. This infinite freedom, ringing out across the earth the permission to live again.

But they were happy with their box.

And so, the finite judged the infinite and chose to live contained.

Little knowing that this expanse of freedom could never be enclosed.

And this grace filled One,

Would never stop showing people the sky.

So who is Jesus?

Jesus is the one who shows us the sky.

Something to consider

The Pharisees could not let go of their tightly held perceptions about the way things should be.

The deep sadness in this story is that they clung on to their misconceptions. In so doing, they boxed themselves in and moved themselves away from saving grace. The very grace that would have set them free.

Sometimes we are like them. But the good news is, Jesus never stops showing us the sky. He never stops beckoning us into freedom broad and wide.

Something to pray

My Jesus, please help me. I am often so contained by what I think, or what I have experienced, or what I assume to be true. Sometimes I get it really wrong.

But you are vast and your forgiveness and freedom are wider than I can imagine. Please help me leave my box tight thinking. Please help me walk in your saving grace. Please show me the sky. Amen.

day 18
the kinship
of
belonging

"…There was a crowd sitting around Jesus and someone said, 'Your mother and your brothers are outside asking for you.' Jesus replied, 'Who is my mother? Who are my brothers?' Then he looked at those around him and said: Look, these are my mother and brothers. Anyone who does God's will is my brother and sister and mother.'"
[Mark 3v31-35 NLT]

They huddled close, sitting at the feet of love divine,
Wanting to stay awhile more,
Just to be near heaven on earth.

They understood though, that when it came to matters of family, they were last in line. It was the way things were. For blood runs thicker.
Blood coursing through the generations, passing on lineage in the kinship of belonging.
It was elitism of ilk, and from this they were barred.
Whereas His mother and brothers, had full claim.

But there, in the crowded room, He began to trace a different text.

The story of inheritance, cast wide.
The chronicle of a household, writing the excluded in.
The narrative of redrawn family lines.

For blood runs thicker.
His blood.

Coursing through the generations, passing on lineage in the Kinship of belonging,
Opening up earth to heaven,

Inviting hearts to huddle close and sit at the feet of love divine.

So who is Jesus?

Jesus is the kinship of belonging.

Something to consider

Jesus defines what His family, the family of God, actually is. It is not about those who by birth have an external claim, it is about those who by heart enter in.

Through what Jesus did on the cross, we can enter in. We are invited to the family table, we are given the family name. God's family isn't about shutting people out, it's about welcoming people in. And so we are invited into the kinship of belonging. We are written into the family line.

Something to pray

My Jesus, thank you that you have included me in your family. Thank you that I am forever in the kinship of belonging. Thank you that you welcome me in. I choose to huddle close and sit at the feet of love divine. Amen.

day 19

the painting
of stories

"He taught by using stories, many stories.
'… A farmer planted seed … some of it fell on the road and
the birds ate it. Some fell in the gravel; it sprouted quickly
but didn't put down roots … Some fell in the weeds and
nothing came of it. Some fell on good earth and came up with
a flourish, producing a harvest exceeding his wildest dreams
… You've been given insight into God's kingdom … But to
those who can't see it yet, everything comes in stories, creating
readiness, nudging them toward receptive insight…'"
[Mark 4v1-20 The Message]

The great storyteller began to set the scene.
Painting thought with His words.
Coating the intangible in the colours of imagination, so bit by bit they could begin to see…

A farmer. A seed. A field.

They held their breath for every brushstroke. Seeing the unfolding, as he painted mystery in hues bright and bold.

Painting onto the canvas of their present, the tones of eternity.
Illuminating their earthen days, with glimpses of the beyond.
So bit by bit they could begin to see…

The farmer. The seed. Their field.

Nudging them towards eyes open, hearts open, lives open
To be painted with the tones of eternity,
To display the colours of mystery, in hues bright and bold.

So who is Jesus?

Jesus is the painter of stories.

Something to consider

Jesus loved to paint truths of the kingdom onto the canvas of story. In the hope that we might be nudged towards receptiveness. So that bit by bit, we can begin to see.

Here, the farmer gives what is precious. A seed. And the desire of the farmer is that the seed would grow. Leaving us wondering about the state of the field.

Leaving me wondering if the seed of God's word can do its work in me?

For if the field of my heart is receptive then the seed will always do its work, bringing the life of the harvest.

Something to pray

My Jesus, I love it that you told stories to help me understand, to help me know you more. This story makes me think about the state of my heart, and I pray that you would help my heart be good soil. Please clear away the things that would choke, or steal the seed of your Word. Help my life go down deep in you. May your word do its work in me. Amen.

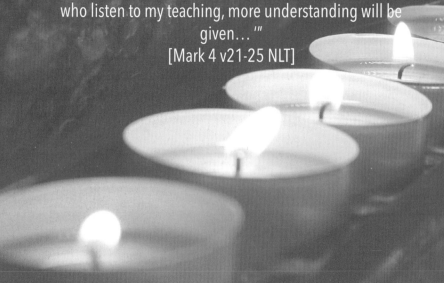

day 20
the light of
listening

"Then Jesus asked them, 'Would anyone light a lamp and
then put it under a basket or under a bed? Of course not!
A lamp is placed on a stand, where its light will shine… '
Then he added, 'Pay close attention to what you hear.
The closer you listen, the more understanding you will
be given – and you will receive even more. To those
who listen to my teaching, more understanding will be
given…'"
[Mark 4 v21-25 NLT]

Lean close and Listen in. Listen deep.
Listen wide.
And in the listening discover light.

Light to pierce darkness. Light to blaze
the way. Light to illuminate the soul.

For it's not about the hiding, it's about
the finding.
So lean close and listen in.

To the light appearing in the timbre of
His voice,
The light revealed in the resonance of
His words,
The light dressed in flesh and speaking
sound.

The sound of light.

Lean close and listen in. Listen deep.
Listen wide

And discover the light of listening.

So who is Jesus?

Jesus is the sound of light.

Something to consider

Jesus is not trying to be obscure. He
wants us to see, He wants us to find,
that's why he came. And the more we
hear, the more we will hear. The more
we see, the more we will see.

Light and sound in the natural both
captivate. I don't know much about
the science of it all, but I do know that
when we are captivated by Him, we
lean in close. Then we will hear more.
Then we will see more.

Something to pray

My Jesus, beautiful bringer of light.
Thank you that your words are light to
my soul. I am leaning in and listening
close. Thank you for what I have already
heard, help me hear more. Thank you
for what I have already seen, help
me see more. I long to be captivated
afresh with you. Amen.

day 21
seed time
and harvest

"Jesus also said, 'The Kingdom of God is like a farmer who scatters seed on the ground. Night and day, while he's asleep or awake, the seed sprouts and grows, but he does not understand how it happens. The earth produces the crops on its own. First a leaf blade pushes through, then the heads of wheat are formed, and finally the grain ripens…'"
[Mark 4 v26-29 NLT]

And then He talked about the kingdom like…

A Seed
Planted in the pleated folds of press and crush,
The gravelling grit of earthen days.

A seed
Persistent in the silted soil of hollow and ridge,
The grime and dust of muddied terrain.

A seed
Concealed in clods of clay.
Deposited deep and ever at work.
Pressing up, pressing through.
Sprouting, spurting, leafing into Fullness.

For the potency of the harvest,
Is held within
A Seed.

So who is Jesus?

Jesus is the substance of the seed.

Something to consider

The seed is made of exactly the right substance, the right stuff, to bring the right harvest. For that is the way with seeds. So it is with the things of God. God's kingdom life, purpose and promise will come to fullness because they are inherently made of the right stuff.

The amazing thing is, God plants the seed of His kingdom within us earthen ones. And the most reassuring thing is, the seed is always at work.

It makes me wonder – do I trust the power of God's seed to be at work in my life, even in the grit and soil of my earthen days? Do I trust the power of God's seed to be at work in other people, even if I can't yet see the harvest?

For the potential of the harvest is held within the seed.

Something to pray

My Jesus, you have planted the seed of your kingdom in this clod of clay! Thank you that you are committed to your kingdom purposes coming about in my life. In the things I can't yet see, I trust you are at work. I trust your seed to bring the right harvest in my life. So, may your kingdom come and your will be done in this earth, and in this particular earthen field. Amen.

day 22
small
beginnings

"Jesus said, 'How can I describe the Kingdom of God? What
story should I use to illustrate it? It is like a mustard seed
planted in the ground. It is the smallest of all seeds, but
it becomes the largest of all garden plants; it grows long
branches, and birds can make nests in its shade…'"
[Mark 4v30-34 NLT]

He began to talk of small beginnings.

Things not grand in glamour, but placed on the minor scale.
Set in the margins. Hidden in the hardly visible. Often dismissed.

Things that are seeded small,
Like a baby in a manger.

Things that are seeded small,
Like the message of God's kingdom told on a carpenter's tongue,
Like a band of unlikely lads appointed and called,
Like a harsh death on an unyielding cross,
Ushering in Ever-increasing,
Ever-reaching Life
For the salvation of us all.

Things that are seeded small.

Divine things.
Becoming the Ever-increasing things,
From glory to glory.

So who is Jesus?

Jesus is the one who seeds things small.

Something to consider

We can often dismiss the divine working of God by thinking it is too small. Too small to notice, too small for our attention. We like the spectacular, whereas God often seeds His kingdom in the small.

Maybe spend a little time noticing the small beginnings of what God is doing in you. Thank God for those things seeded small. And why not dare to believe that God, who seeded them, will bring them to fullness.

Something to pray

My Jesus, thank you that you never dismiss the small beginnings in me. Thank you for the things you have seeded small in my heart. Please come and breathe upon them, so they can grow and blossom into fullness, giving life to others and glorifying your name. Amen.

day 23
lakes & boats

"'Let's cross to the other side of the lake.' So they took Jesus in the boat and started out … But soon a fierce storm came up. High waves were breaking into the boat, and it began to fill with water. Jesus was sleeping at the back of the boat with his head on a cushion. The disciples woke him up, shouting 'Teacher, don't you care that we're going to drown?' When Jesus woke up, he rebuked the wind and said to the waves, 'Silence! Be still!' Suddenly the wind stopped, and there was a great calm … 'Who is this man?' they asked each other. 'Even the wind and waves obey him!'" [Mark 4v35-41 NLT]

Lakes and boats. Boats and lakes.

This was their terrain, and they knew the water well.
They could read the liquid patterns, they could trace the spray and swirl,
They had been lords of this landscape since early days.

But this time was different. This time they were afraid.

They stared into the ever-expanding eye of the storm
And the crash and the gush, smashed through every steady space,
And the mass and the rush, collided in blow upon deafening blow.
Oceanic in its drenching,
Breaking right over the edge,
Tipping them into turbulence.

Then He spoke
Words like oil on troubled waters.
Words like balm on troubled souls.

For he was Lord of every landscape,
And he could calm every storm.

So who is Jesus?

Jesus is the storm-calmer.

Something to consider

Sometimes we are all at sea. We feel overwhelmed, like the next wave might sink us. Sometimes the continuous blows have left us gasping for survival, crying out to God, and wondering why He seems to be asleep.

One thing I love about this story is that Jesus always intended the disciples to get to the other side. He intends us to get to the other side too.

I also love that Jesus was there with them. Even though they couldn't understand what was gong on, they were safe in His care. We are too.

And then I love how Jesus speaks peace into the outward storm, and peace into the inward storm. He wants to do that for us too.

Something to pray

My Jesus, you have brought me through many storms and I am so grateful. I need you right in the centre of what I am facing. Please come and speak peace to the outward, and speak peace to the inward. I trust you will bring me through. I know you are with me. I know you are Lord. I know you are the one who will calm this storm. Amen.

day 24
storms
brewing

" … As Jesus got out of the boat, a madman from the cemetery came up to him. He lived there among the tombs and the graves. No one could restrain him … Night and day he roamed through the graves and the hills, screaming out and slashing himself with sharp stones …

Jesus asked him, "Tell me your name." He replied, "My name is Mob. I'm a rioting mob."

… They came up to Jesus and saw the madman sitting there wearing decent clothes and making sense … As Jesus was getting into the boat, the demon-delivered man begged to go along … Jesus said, "Go home to your own people. Tell them your story … "" [Mark 5v1-20 The Message]

The fisherlads had survived one storm, but now they encountered a tempest of a different kind.

One ravaging the heart of a man.

It was a cyclone of unrest, advancing in riotous anarchy,

Demanding total occupation,

Casting chaos into every fragile space.

The man was left shackled in the wreck.

Naked in the ruins. With the will to live battered right down.

And it was him that the once upon a carpenter, had come to find…

The man had never been so clean clothed
In every fragile space.

And he fell at the feet of

The Liberator

In peaceful soundness of mind.

So who is Jesus?

Jesus is the Liberator.

Something to consider

It is the Liberator who understand the [...] of freedom. And for each of us, there are different things we may find ourselves trapped in. They might not be as extreme as they were for this man, but they can bring torment and pain.

Jesus is still the liberator. He wants us to be free, and He comes to heal the tempest-filled places in our hearts.

The great thing about this story is that the once bound, now becomes a storyteller within God's incredible narrative. The man begins to tell of mercy and grace. He begins to tell others about freedom.

Something to pray

Jesus my Liberator, thank you that you bring order into chaos. Thank you that you are my restorer and my healer. Please come and bring your freedom into all the tempest-filled places of my heart. Amen.

day 25

rewriting
the lines

"…A woman who had suffered a condition of haemorrhaging for twelve years … had heard about Jesus … She was thinking to herself, 'If I can put a finger on his robe, I can get well.' The moment she did it, the flow of blood dried up … At the same moment, Jesus felt energy discharging from him. He turned around to the crowd and asked, 'Who touched my robe?' … he went on asking, looking around to see who had done it … Jesus said to her, 'Daughter you took a risk of faith, and now you're healed and whole…'"
[Mark 5 v21-34 The Message]

She'd watched it all seep away. Like sewage.

Life, discarded in the discharge. Life, cast in the relentless dash of hope and smash of sorrow. Year on year. On repeat.

Sometimes the script looked like it might be redrawn, and for a brief moment she surfaced. Only to be typecast back in the old role, repeating lines forever written in her lifeblood.

It would have been easy to withdraw to the edge, but there was something about this carpenter turned preacher man!

She didn't need him to see her, she just had to get to him. So she stalked the shadows, edging her way near, just to touch

The tip

Of his robe.

He stopped. Everyone was confused. There were more pressing matters at hand, but he would not budge.

She was exposed.

And there, on redemption's stage, He began to redefine her role.

Dignifying her in the discharge, Casting her within the relentless flow of grace, Re-wording her script and rewriting her lines.

So who is Jesus?

Jesus is the rewriter of lines.

Something to consider

This woman took a risk of faith that changed everything. She had good reason to give up, but she didn't. She just needed to get to Jesus.

In her boldness of faith, she found the grace of Jesus to rewrite and redefine her story.

I wonder, are there areas of life where it's time to take a faith risk? A faith risk based on who He is, and what He has said. If so, may we have boldness like this woman. And may we know that if we even touch the very edge of who He is, everything can change.

Something to pray

My Jesus, thank you that with you everything can change, even situations that have been going on for a long time. Help me live bold in my faith. Help me keep expecting amazing things because of who you are. Come and redefine my story. I'm pressing through and touching even the edge of you today, because my deepest hope is you. Amen.

marking time

"'Your daughter is dead. Why bother the Teacher any more?'
Jesus overheard what they were talking about and said to the
leader, 'Don't listen to them; just trust me.' … when he had
sent them all out, he took the child's father and mother along
with his companions, and entered the child's room. He clasped
the girl's hand and said, 'Talitha koum,' which means, 'Little
girl, get up.' At that she was up and walking around!"
[Mark 5v35-43 the Message]

Each second holding life and death in the balance,
Each breath pushing forward each move of the dial, marking time.
Marking the running out, and the running into sorrow deep.

He was their last hope.

And then the news came. The stuff of life gave way, for the balance had been
tipped. And time. Stood. Still.

But the once upon a carpenter, did not think it was over just yet.
They huddled in the room, confronted by breath stopped. Life stopped. Full stop.
And he picked up her cooling hand.

His words, more weighty than death's heavy claim,
Shifting the balance.

Each breath pushing forwards,
Each breath marking time,
Each breath running into life

Given by The Life Bringer.

So who is Jesus?

Jesus is the Life Bringer.

Something to consider

Sometimes things seem over and dead, whether that is a dream, a promise, a hope…

Here, Jesus brought the little girl back to life. It was impossible yet possible. Today, Jesus can still bring life into our impossibilities. Even the ones that seem dead.

What do you need to ask God to breathe his life into? Because He is still healer, restorer, and the bringer of Life. And you never know, miracles might be waiting!

Something to pray

My Jesus, you the one filled with life. You can bring life even into impossible things. Please come into the stuff of my impossible, for you can do anything, for you are the life bringer. I trust you, and look to you to see how you will bring life right in. Amen.

day 27
against
the grain

"Jesus … returned with his disciples to Nazareth, his hometown. The next Sabbath he began teaching in the synagogue, and many who heard him were amazed. They asked, 'Where did he get all this wisdom and the power to perform such miracles?' Then they scoffed, 'He's just a carpenter, the son of Mary and the brother of James, Joseph, Judas, and Simon. And his sisters live right here among us.' They were deeply offended and refused to believe in him."
[Mark 6v1-6 NLT]

He grew up amongst the dust,
The sawdust of a carpenter's trade.

In the chop of wood and plane of tool,
He was one of them.
With life carved out in the sweat and
the groove
And the form of the future already
engraved,
He was like them.
They could trace the markings of his
mother in the lines of his face,
They knew him.

But here he was, talking of higher
things,
Daring to go against the grain.

They were affronted and splintered
through with assumption,
So they swept wisdom away like
useless wood-shave.
And He was staggered
At how much they missed

Because they wouldn't see against the
grain.

So who is Jesus?

Jesus is the one who goes against the
grain.

Something to consider

Sometimes we can feel dismissed
when people don't really understand
the journey, or see what God has put
within us.

But God always knows, He always sees,
and He will always see to it.

Jesus' life wasn't limited by people's
perceptions of who He was, or who He
wasn't. Jesus trusted the Father and
lived true to Himself – even though
that was against the grain. We can live
true to who the Father has made us,
trusting our way to Him with a yielded
heart, because He knows, He sees, and
He will see to it.

Something to pray

Beautiful Jesus, thank you that you
lived bold and free in truth. Help me
live true to what you have placed
within me. Also, please help me to
see others as you see them, to see the
beauty within.

I trust you. Thank you that you know,
thank you that you see, thank you that
you will see to it. Amen.

day 28
the run of things

"Jesus called the Twelve to him, and sent them out in pairs. He gave them authority and power to deal with the evil opposition. He sent them off … Then they were on the road. They preached with joyful urgency that life can be radically different; right and left they sent the demons packing; they brought wellness to the sick, anointing their bodies, healing their spirits."
[Mark 6v7-13 The Message]

They were getting used to the run of things, these fisherlads.

He would bring down heaven, they would be in awe. He would teach wisdom, they would be amazed. He would tread the path, they would follow in His steps. But now it was all in the change.

He was sending them out.

Some of the usual suspects had been eager to show the world. But now it came to it, they were faced with their own lack and wondered if they would be enough.

Yet, He was sending them, so out they went into the new run of things.

Where they would bring down heaven, they would teach wisdom, they would tread His path. And others would follow in His steps.

For He would be enough for them,
And they would be undaunted
In His Name.

So who is Jesus?

Jesus is the one who sends us.

Something to consider

The disciples knew they were called, but now they were actually being sent. They weren't just meant to observe the story, they were meant to participate in it.

On the way, they discovered that Jesus would be enough for them in the adventure He was calling them to. For, they were carriers of His name and bringers of His life. And so are we.

Why not spend a bit of time asking Jesus where He wants to send you to be a carrier of His life … it could be as simple as down the street.

Wherever He sends you He will be with you, and He will be enough for you.

Something to pray

My Jesus, thank you that you don't want me to just be an observer of your story, you have a part for me to play in your story. Please show me where you want me to be a carrier of your life, so that others may discover you and encounter your freedom. Amen.

day 29
word on
the street

"Herod Antipas, the king, soon heard about Jesus, because everyone was talking about him. Some were saying, 'This must be John the Baptist raised from the dead. That is why he can do such miracles.' Others said, 'He's a prophet like the other great prophets of the past.'"
[Mark 6v14-30 NLT]

The word on the street,
Spreading speculation,
Layering guess upon
Supposition,
In the try of articulation…
Who is this man?

Rumour on rumour,
Airing assertion,
Debating back and forth
Allegation,
In the hunt of investigation…
Who is this man?

Half light reporting,
Claiming conclusion,
Full light beholding and
Conviction,
In the joy of consolidation…
(Who is) This Man!

So who is Jesus?

Jesus is one who invokes response.

Something to consider

The news of Jesus was spreading everywhere. Causing people to ask, 'Who is this man?' The reports even arrived at the palace door, reminding Herod of dark days and blood on his hands.

Jesus' walk with God was joy to many, and anguish to some. But His life always invoked a response, inviting people to come and find out for themselves.

May the report of our lives, and our adventure with God, cause other people to ask, 'Who is this Jesus?' Because then they might discover more of Him.

Something to pray

My Jesus, thank you that you are always inviting response, so that people might find out for themselves who you really are.

May my life be so filled with your life, your adventure in me, your beauty, your love, that it causes others to want to know 'Who is this Jesus?' Amen.

the reach

"Then Jesus said, 'Lets go off by ourselves to a quiet place and rest awhile.' Jesus saw the huge crowd as he stepped from the boat, and he had compassion on them because they were like sheep without a shepherd. So he began teaching them many things … Late in the afternoon his disciples came to him and said … 'Send the crowds away so they can … buy something to eat.' But Jesus said, 'You feed them.' … Jesus took the five loaves and two fish, looked up toward heaven, and blessed them. Then, breaking the loaves into pieces, he kept giving the bread to the disciples so they could distribute it to the people … A total of 5,000 men and their families were fed."
[Mark 6v30-44 NLT]

They were at the end of the day, the end of the stretch,
Expecting quiet, but instead got the noise of a multitude.

His heart was wide enough for them all but theirs were slightly running out of space. Expiring in the giving and the sharing and the herding like shepherds, Reaching the line between the steady and the plummet.

They were on the brink of that void so empty, at the edge of the end,
The end of themselves.

Sending the bleating away was the only conclusion for they had nothing to give. But He had other ideas.

He took the little, blessed the brokenness and gave it out.

And at the end of the day, at the edge of the end, they stepped into
The Reach of
Nothing
But
God.

It was enough for them all.

So who is Jesus?

Jesus is the reach.

Something to consider

The disciples must have been confronted with their lack of ability to bring the answer, and it must have been overwhelming. It's that panic of when your resource, ability, and strength have reached their limit. There is no way that you can make the way. However, when we come to the end of ourselves, we step into the reach of Nothing But God.

On this day, the multitude feasted on a picnic of provision, with food left over. For Jesus was the reach between their impossibility and God's ability. He still is.

Maybe we can give thanks for the little bits of good, place them in Jesus' hands, and see God do the impossible.

Something to pray

Beautiful Jesus, thank you that when I feel at the end of myself, I am perfectly positioned for your miraculous.

Thank you for the little pockets of good I see. I give them to you and pray you would bless them and multiply them. I ask for your miraculous provision and breakthrough. Thank you that you are the reach between my impossibilities and all of the ability of the Godhead. Amen.

Space to Think...

day 31
safe to shore

"Late that night, the disciples were in their boat in the middle of the lake, and Jesus was alone on land. He saw that they were in serious trouble, rowing hard and struggling against the wind and waves. About three o'clock in the morning Jesus came toward them, walking on the water … 'Don't be afraid,' he said. 'Take courage! I am here!' Then he climbed into the boat, and the wind stopped. They were totally amazed, for they still didn't understand the significance of the miracle of the loaves."
[Mark 6v 45-56 NLT]

They were stuck in the strain of the silent hours,
Pulling hard against the push of the elements,
Struggling to stay afloat, struggling to understand,
Struggling with all they had seen.

Bread from heaven. A mirror of miracles from long ago days, when God revealed himself to his people: The Yesterday. The Today. The Forever. The Same.

But the memory was fading in the wash of unyielding waves,
And now it was the fourth watch of the night, the third hour of the new day, and still they were fighting against the sea. Adrift and alone.

Then He was there.
Speaking reassurance, like dawn spreading gold across the waters. Like faith stirring courage from the depths. Like peace rolling relief into the silent hours.

The Yesterday. The Today. The Forever. The Same

Bringing them Safe to Shore.

So who is Jesus?

Jesus is The Yesterday. The Today. The Forever. The Same.

Something to consider

The disciples had been struggling through a whole lot of dark hours, where Jesus was not obviously there, but they were obviously in trouble.
Jesus saw they were struggling, he came to them, he spoke to them, and then the wind stopped. But we are told that the disciples were amazed because they "still didn't understand the significance of the miracle of the loaves."

So what was it within the miracle of the loaves that was meant to carry them through the silent hours of straining at the oars? What were they meant to be remembering?
Maybe it was something about the character of God: The Yesterday. The Today. The Forever. The Same.
And it makes me wonder, what am I meant to be remembering about God that will lead me through my present hours and cause my heart to take courage?

Something to pray

My Jesus, thank you that I am safe with you, even in the times where it seems I am straining through the silent hours. I remember who you are. I remember what you have done. Thank you that you are The Yesterday. The Today. The Forever. The Same. I know you will bring me safe to shore. Amen.

day 32
fine
china living

"One day some Pharisees and
teachers of religious law arrived
from Jerusalem to see Jesus.
They noticed that some of his
disciples failed to follow the Jewish
ritual of hand washing before eating.
(… This is but one of many traditions
they have clung to - such as their
ceremonial washing of cups,
pitchers, and kettles.)
… Jesus replied, 'You hypocrites!
Isaiah was right when he prophesied
about you for he wrote, "These people
honour me with their lips,
but their hearts are far from me…"'"
[Mark 7v1-23 NLT]

Jesus is True of Heart.

Something to consider

The Pharisees loved the appearance of perfection, whereas Jesus was True of Heart.

Jesus was much firmer on the Pharisees, who thought they were so righteous, than on people who knew they needed forgiveness. For the Pharisees were not living in truth. The Pharisees' honour of God had been reduced to lip service. Their worship had been replaced with rules. And the words of God ignored in favour of the traditions of man. It meant their honour was worthless, their worship meaningless, and their tradition useless.

Jesus calls us to be true of heart, but how much are we like the Pharisees? It is a challenge, which causes me to pray, 'Jesus, create in me a clean heart.'

Something to pray

My Jesus, I am so sorry for when I have been fooled by the appearance of things, when I have put so much energy into what is fake. I want my life to be of true substance. I long to have a true heart.

Thank you that you are the one who forgives and cleans me from the inside out. Please create in the depths of me a clean heart. Amen.

Their exhibit was a whole collection of
Fine china living.
Polished and Pristine,
Passed down the generations
In artful assortments of
Shine and Glaze.

Their lives, a cabinet display of
Porcelain Perfection.
Good for a spectacle,
But holding
No
Substance.

He was not impressed with their
coverings of gloss.
For He could see
All
The
Cracks.

day 33
outrageous grace

"Then Jesus … went north to the region of Tyre … Right away a woman who had heard about him came and fell at his feet. Her little girl was possessed by an evil spirit, and she begged him to cast out the demon from her daughter. Since she was a Gentile … Jesus told her, 'First I should feed the children – my own family, the Jews. It isn't right to take food from the children and throw it to the dogs.' She replied, 'That's true Lord, but even the dogs under the table are allowed to eat the scraps from the children's plates.' 'Good answer!' he said. 'Now go home, for the demon has left your daughter.'"
[Mark 7v24-30 NLT]

She knew she shouldn't be there.

Her culture and custom were cut from the wrong cloth,
Her birth-right, a brand of exclusion.
And to be near one who seamed the tear between God and man…
You first, had to be sown with the right thread.
She was not. And they All knew it.

And yet in she came, right to his feet.

He followed the prescribed pattern. But somewhere into the cut of words, He gave her hope. She said she was only asking for a scrap, she didn't presume on a rolled out measure, but even a scrap would be enough. For everything!

He delighted in her answer, delighted in her faith,
Delighted in re-patterning the order of things.
Hemming her in, with outrageous grace,
Pleat upon pleat,
Stitch upon stitch,
Seaming the tear between
God and man.

So who is Jesus?

Jesus is the bringer of outrageous grace.

Something to consider

This woman knew that even a crumb of Jesus' mercy, a scrap of his grace, a tiny part of His power, would be enough to bring a complete miracle.

She did not expect more than a scrap, because of her position and her race. However Jesus rolled out mercy in vast measure. He delighted in welcoming her. For His purpose is always to mend the tear between God and man, to fill that gap with outrageous grace.

Sometimes we can feel like we do not have the right labels to qualify for God's love. Whether that is because of our history, our culture, our class, our anything. But Jesus is the bringer of outrageous grace.

Something to pray

Beautiful Jesus, thank you that you offer me outrageous grace. Grace to heal, grace to restore, grace to forgive, grace to cover, grace for me to be connected back to you. Thank you for your grace. By your grace I have boldness to believe for miracles, and by your grace I can come close to you. I gladly receive your grace and am forever grateful. Amen.

face to face

"… A deaf man with a speech impediment was brought to him … Jesus led him away from the crowd so they could be alone. He put his fingers into the man's ears. Then spitting on his own fingers, he touched the man's tongue. Looking up to heaven, he sighed and said, 'Ephphatha,' which means, 'Be opened!' Instantly the man could hear perfectly, and his tongue was freed so he could speak plainly!" [Mark 7v31-37 NLT]

Leaving the crowded agenda and the chased-after spectacle, far behind.
Now drawn close.

Eye to eye. Face to face.

Alone
With his
Maker.

Drawn into the still
Of nothing to hide and nothing to fear.

Drawn into the dawn
Of new creation.

Eye to eye. Face to face.

Alone
With his
Maker.

So who is Jesus?

Jesus is the one who draws us close.

Something to consider

The crowds were hungry for the spectacular, but Jesus drew the man aside for encounter.

Sometimes we are so fascinated by the show of things, that we miss the moments of intimacy. Those moments where God wants to draw us close and breathe new life. Where we are face to face with Him. Where we are drawn into that place of encounter. May we not rush past those precious moments!

Maybe it is time to draw aside with Jesus, into the still of nothing to hide and nothing to fear, and there encounter Him bringing new creation.

Something to pray

My Jesus, I long to draw close enough to hear your whisper. Amen.

day 35
opening the
storehouse
wide

"…another large crowd had gathered, and the people ran out of food again. Jesus called his disciples and told them, 'I feel sorry for these people. They have been here with me for three days, and they have nothing left to eat…' His disciples replied, 'How are we supposed to find enough food to feed them out here in the wilderness?' Jesus answered, 'How much bread do you have?' 'Seven loaves' … Afterward, the disciples picked up seven large baskets of leftover food. There were about 4,000 people in the crowd that day…"
[Mark 8v1-10 NLT]

There was something about it that was all too familiar.

The once upon a fisherlads, stood in the confinement of resource run dry. Again. Their stores only stuffed with air.

He had done it before, but would he this time? Could he this time? Or had provision reached its peak with the five and the two?
Had they had their portion?

The hungry ones sat down in expectancy,
All ready. All waiting.

Then in the blessedness
of this bread broken,
of His life broken,

He opened the store house wide.

It was filled to the brim, filled to the overflow, filled with abundance of Heaven-sent supply.

So who is Jesus?

Jesus is the one who opens the storehouse wide.

Something to consider

I have often wondered why this story was included in the gospels, because it is almost an exact repeat of the feeding of the 5,000. But maybe that is the point. Maybe God wanted to say it loud and clear that His mercy, His grace, His power, His provision is always in abundance. We never reach the end of it, we never reach the end of Him. His love and goodness never run out on us.
The storehouse, of everything He is, is always open wide.

Something to pray

My Jesus, I cannot even begin to get my head around the fact that your love does not run out. I am overwhelmed that I never reach the limit of the goodness you want to pour into my life. I come to you with no entitlement and no demand, but a deep knowing and expectancy that you are good and you do good. My Jesus I ask and wait for your heaven-sent supply. Amen.

day 36

trust on
trial

"When the Pharisees heard that Jesus had arrived, they came and started
to argue with him. Testing him, they demanded that he show them a
miraculous sign from heaven to prove his authority. When he heard this,
he sighed deeply in his spirit, 'Why do these people keep demanding a
miraculous sign? I tell you the truth, I will not give this generation any
such sign.'"
[Mark 8v11-13 NLT]

They entered costumed as judge and juror,
Onto the platform
Of refute and rebuttal,
Of dispute and disclaim.

Buttoned up in entitlement.
Demanding their way.

They gave their opening lines and squabbled it out in accusation,
Robed with the assumption that they had
Every
Right.

As if the earthen, could stage the Holy
On trial.

And he sighed at their ill-judged script.

Desiring trust
Not
Demand.

So who is Jesus?

Jesus is the one who desires trust.

Something to consider

It's easy to criticise the Pharisees from the perspective of who we know Jesus to be... How foolish of them to think that they had authority to demand God to do their bidding! How arrogant, to command Jesus to prove Himself!

And yet, how often do echoes of those demands come out of our own hearts? How often do we put God on trial when things haven't worked out the way we wanted them to? When we expect Him to orchestrate situations in accordance with the way we have scripted the play? When we want Him to prove Himself to us?

Instead of entitlement and demand, Jesus desires trust. He beckons us to trust. To trust His power, trust His love, trust His goodness, trust who He is.
Because it is those things that are trustworthy.

Maybe it's time to lay entitlement aside, and trust again.

Something to pray

My Jesus, I am so sorry for when I come to you in demand and entitlement, based on how I want things to go. I'm sorry for all of that, and instead choose to trust. I trust you are good, I trust you are for me, I trust all you did on the cross, I trust who you are. You are my hope forever. Amen.

day 37
clear
sight

"As they were crossing the lake, Jesus warned them,
'Watch out! Beware of the yeast of the Pharisees and
of Herod.' At this they began to argue with each other
because they hadn't brought any bread ... 'Why are
you arguing about having no bread? Don't you know or
understand even yet? Are your hearts too hard to take it
in? You have eyes – can't you see? You have ears – can't
you hear? Don't you remember anything at all?
When I fed the 5,000 with five loaves of bread, how many
baskets of leftovers did you pick up afterward?"
[Mark 8v13-21 NLT]

They got into the boat with the once upon a carpenter, the one who held more mystery than they could see.

He was not happy about something, but they could not grasp its measure with any clarity.

Blurred in mistake
Turned to blame.

Blinkered in the
Fret of distraction.

Blinded in misconception.

Walking with their eyes shut, they were among the sightless.

So He nudged them to refocus,
And called them into

Clear sight.

So who is Jesus?

Jesus is the one who calls us into clear sight.

Something to consider

Sometimes we get so distracted by the immediate stuff of life that we don't see what is really going on.

The disciples completely missed the point that Jesus was making about the contamination of the Pharisees' heart attitude. They also had completely forgotten that Jesus could provide for them if they didn't have enough lunch.

They were caught up in their own agenda and so failed to see clearly. Sometimes we are like that too.

Maybe it's time to ask God for clarity concerning your situation and believe that He will show you what is really going on, and what He is really saying.

Something to pray

My Jesus, thank you that you can bring clarity into every situation I face. Please help me get my eyes off the distractions, and off the immediate stuff that might be confusing my understanding. Help me to see with clear sight. Amen.

the
illuminate

"Jesus took the blind man by the hand and led him out of the village. Then, spitting on the man's eyes, he laid his hands on him and asked, 'Can you see anything now?' The man looked around, 'Yes,' he said, 'I see people but I can't see them very clearly…' Then Jesus placed his hands on the man's eyes again, and his eyes were opened. His sight was completely restored, and he could see everything clearly."
[Mark 8v22-26 NLT]

Heavy Dark.

Fist thick,
Blanket thick,
Spreading over every edge
In heavy suffocation.

Covering each corner with
Dark,
Tucking him tight into the
BLACKOUT.

Then He came by.
Peeling darkness back with a flicker, then a tint,
Then a tinge, then a flare,
Then a Blaze of Light.

Till heavy dark was undone.

And he could bask in the
ILLUMINATE.

So who is Jesus?

Jesus is the illuminate.

Something to consider

This man had lived life one way, for a long time. Physical darkness was his normal. He probably found lots of ways to make the most out of things, but ultimately he wanted to see. Jesus gave the physical ability to see, and then the man had a new normal.

I love that Jesus wants to create a new normal in our lives, whether that is physical, emotional, or spiritual. I also love that this miracle was done bit by bit, as it reminds me that God's miracles can happen like that too.

Maybe take a little time to ask God for His light to increase, and increase again, into all the dark and heavy areas of life. Believing He will begin to create a new normal. He will bring the illuminate.
And may we celebrate each step of the miracle as it unfolds!

Something to pray

Beautiful Jesus, thank you that you are the light bringer. May your light increase more and more into every corner of my heart so I can live fully in your illuminate. Amen.

beginning to see

"…As they were walking along, he asked them, 'Who do people say I am?'
'Well,' they replied, 'some say John the Baptist, some say Elijah, and
others say you are one of the other prophets.' Then he asked them, 'But
who do you say I am?' Peter replied, 'You are the Messiah.'
[Mark 8v27-30 NLT]

The story was unfolding…

With every path walked out, and every moment breathed in,
With miracles made real on flesh, and words made real in hearts,
With meals shared, days shared, life shared,

And they were beginning to see

God's love lived in skin.

He held the age-old pieces together,
All that had gone before, All that was to come,
Making the door between heaven and earth,
Opening eternity wide.

And they
Were beginning
To see

God's love lived in skin.

So who is Jesus?

Jesus is God's love lived in skin.

Something to consider

This moment marked a turning point for the disciples and for Jesus' focus throughout the rest of the Gospel. The disciples had spent days, and even a couple of years, getting to know this carpenter turned preacher man. And after all they had seen, all they had heard, they needed to decide for themselves who Jesus was. Was He just a man? Was He just a prophet? Or was He the Messiah - God's rescue for us all?

Peter declared that Jesus was the Christ, the Messiah, the one from God who would save.

At this point, it is good to ask ourselves who do we know Jesus to be?
If you have never welcomed Jesus into your life as Christ and friend, this could be your time. It doesn't need fancy words, it just needs a prayer from the heart speaking out who Jesus is, saying sorry for the things that have separated you from God, trusting Jesus' rescue, and inviting Him to be Lord and leader of your own life. It will be the turning point, for Jesus opens the door between heaven and earth wide.

Something to pray

Jesus, thank you that you are the Christ, God Himself, who came to rescue us all. I trust in you. I am sorry for the things that have separated me from you and I trust in your rescue. I welcome you as Lord and Christ of my life. Thank you that I am forever yours. Thank you that you have opened the door between heaven and earth wide for me. Amen.

day 40
the way of
the cross

"Then Jesus began to tell them that the Son of Man must suffer many
terrible things … He would be killed, but three days later he would
rise from the dead … Then calling the crowd to join his disciples, he
said, 'If any of you wants to be my follower, you must turn from your
selfish ways, take up your cross, and follow me. If you try to hang on to
your life, you will lose it. But if you give up your life for my sake and for
the sake of the good news, you will save it.'"
[Mark 8v31-38 NLT]

They had arrived at the edge of before and after,
And the once upon a carpenter began bracing them for The Cross Beam.

That weight bearing, ego tearing beam,
Nailed through with surrender.

The cross beam of taking it up and laying it down,
Marking the divide between
Self
and
Abandon.

The crossing beam of
Life
and
Death.

His cross beam.
Becoming their crossing beam.
Becoming their cross beam
And the axis for everything after.

So who is Jesus?

Jesus is the one who embraced the Cross Beam.

Something to consider

This was the first time Jesus told His disciples about His imminent death, and through this, He laid out what it really means to follow Him. To walk the way of heart surrender. To embrace the cross beam.

We often don't like the idea of surrender, we want things our way. But Jesus said that the way to life is not in holding onto our own life, our own way, our own control, our own agenda, our own anything… but holding onto Him.
For when we really surrender, we find His life waiting on the other side.

Something to pray

My Jesus, thank you that you were willing to walk the way of the cross for me. Thank you that by your death, I have life. Thank you that you now call me to walk with you, on this journey of heart surrender. I let go my hold on anything I am clinging to too tightly. I trust your goodness, and I believe you will bring life on the other side of surrender. Amen.

see
deeper

"…Jesus took Peter, James, and John, and led them up a high mountain to be alone. As the men watched, Jesus' appearance was transformed, and his clothes became dazzling white, far whiter than any earthly bleach could ever make them… Then a cloud overshadowed them, and a voice from the cloud said, 'This is my dearly loved Son. Listen to him.'"
[Mark 9v1-13 NLT]

The once upon a fisherlads were climbing the mountain again.

These ones covered in the dust of earthen days,
Lifted from lowly shores, lined with the years.

But the lines were being redrawn as they stood in awe.

Breathing in the grandeur of
GLORY.

Breath-taken with the
HOLY.

They stood in humble trembling, and beheld
Brilliance
Thick like a cloud.
Dense like in ages past, when a wondering people met with their God.

And they marvelled at the magnificence,
And they marvelled at the once upon a carpenter,
Now seen as
GLORIOUS.

So who is Jesus?

Jesus is glorious.

Something to consider

The disciples knew Jesus in one way, but now they were being invited to see him deeper. To see Him in His glory. May we never grow so accustomed to 'Jesus the man', that we forget Jesus, Son of God, The Holy One.

Maybe it's time to gaze at Him again and be breath-taken by His splendour, by His beauty, and by the knowledge that He calls us earthen ones close.

Something to pray

Beautiful Jesus, I am in awe of you. You are glorious. You are beautiful. You are robed in splendour and clothed in majesty. I cannot even begin to understand your holiness, your brilliance. I am forever in awe and humbled, that you beckon this earthen one to tread on holy ground. Thank you that you welcome me into your very presence. I am breath-taken by your love and by the grandeur of you. Amen.

day 42
out of chaos

"One of the men in the crowd spoke up and said 'Teacher, I brought
my son ... He is possessed by an evil spirit that won't let him talk. And
whenever the spirit seizes him, it throws him violently to the ground ... So
I asked your disciples to cast out the evil spirit, but they couldn't do it ...
Have mercy on us and help us if you can.' 'What do you mean, "If I can"?'
Jesus asked. 'Anything is possible if a person believes.' The father instantly
cried out 'I do believe, but help me overcome my unbelief!'"
[Mark 9v14-29 NLT]

Down from the mountain, and thick into the clash of
Order and Chaos.

With darkness asserting its clout,
Smashing innocence against its spite,
Basking in its reign of terror.

A battleground contesting rule and reign, in the collision of
Faith and Fear.

The once upon a carpenter does not flinch.

And darkness has to relent, has to consent to a higher rule, a truer reign.
For faith triumphs. Like love triumphs. Like grace triumphs. Like He triumphs.

And All things become possible.

Because the rightful King

Holds the rights.

Jesus is the Rightful King.

Something to consider

The rightful King was coming to set wrong right. To displace darkness' rule, and to bring God's order, God's life, God's light, into the chaos of a broken world.

Darkness had to bow to His authority. It always does.

And in this healing of a little boy, Jesus reveals something more of who He is. And He calls His disciples, and us, to have faith.

Faith in Him. Faith in who He is. Faith in the deeper authority of God.

Because in Him limits are lifted, restrictions removed, and all things become possible.

Maybe today is the day to have faith again.

Something to pray

My Jesus, you are the rightful King. You are the one who brings God's order into chaos.

I put my trust in you, in who you are, in what you have done. And I have faith again for your Kingdom to come into the things I face. For in you all things are possible. Amen.

day 43
the
shadow lands

"Jesus ... wanted to spend more time with his disciples and teach them.
He said to them, 'The Son of Man is going to be betrayed into the hands
of his enemies. He will be killed, but three days later he will rise from
the dead.' They didn't understand what he was saying, however, and they
were afraid to ask him what he meant."
[Mark 9v30-32 NLT]

It was precious time,

Before the journey into the shadow lands began.

That darkened place where sorrow would run deep, like wounds run deep,
like tears run deep, like tares ripping through and carving out cavernous grief
right in the core.

It was precious time.

For these were the moments before.
And He knew it.

These were the moments before.
And He chose it.

So that the wounding and the carving and the tearing
Would lead to the mending and restoring and repairing,

Of us all.

So who is Jesus?

Jesus is the one who entered the shadow lands.

Something to consider

Jesus fully knew what was ahead of Him, and He willing chose to walk the darkest path. He chose the cross. Not running from the sorrow and the grief of it, but running to embrace us through it.

At the cross He owned all the tears ever cried. He carried the cuts of the ages.

And He did it for you and for me.

Something to pray

My Jesus, all I can say is thank you. I will never know the depth of sorrow that you carried on the cross. I will never know what it really cost. But I am forever grateful that you carried my tears. You carried the cuts of the ages. And by your wounds, I am healed. And by your death, I can live.

Thank you that you walked through the shadow lands for my sake, and for the sake of us all. Amen.

day 44

lifting
the least

"… Jesus asked his disciples, 'What were you discussing out on the road?' But they didn't answer, because they had been arguing about which of them was the greatest.
He sat down, called the twelve disciples over to him, and said, 'Whoever wants to be first must take last place and be the servant of everyone else.' Then he put a little child among them. Taking the child in his arms, he said to them, 'Anyone who welcomes a little child like this on my behalf welcomes me, and anyone who welcomes me welcomes not only me but also my Father who sent me.'" [Mark 9v33-37 NLT]

The little one stood in the middle of them,

Seeing safe eyes, safe smile, safe love, and giggling with the whisk into His arms.

For He was treading out a different path, and the ones glazed by their own grandeur were invited to follow.

To abandon the pursuit of splendor, and become like this King,

This One who loved enough to bow low.

For, humble He comes,
Stooping to lift the earthen.

Humble He comes,
To love the least and lift the little.

Humble He comes,
To whisk the lowly into arms deep, heart deep, life deep
In ever-encircling grace.

Treading out the path of

Greatness.

So who is Jesus?

Jesus is the one who loves enough.

Something to consider

Jesus turned all the normal assumptions of greatness, upside down. Or, the right way up!

We get so consumed with our ideas of what it means to be successful, what it means to be great, but God's ideas seem to be very different. They are more clothed in love than prestige. Even in the flourishing things, the exciting things, the prominent things, and the things that are blessed to be on a large scale, they are still more concerned with a humble heart than an outward display of success.

May we love enough to bow a little lower and lift the least.

Something to pray

Beautiful Jesus, you are the One worthy of honour, of praise, and of every accolade. And yet you humbled yourself and poured out love to lift the least. Please forgive me when I get so caught up in what I think is 'great'. Help me see clearly the way things really are. Please help me become more like you, in loving enough to bow a little lower, and to lift the least. Amen.

day 45

salty
words

"'…anyone by just giving you a
cup of water in my name is on
our side. Count on it that God
will notice…' On the other hand,
if you give one of these simple,
childlike believers a hard time,
bullying or taking advantage of
their simple trust, you'll soon wish
you hadn't …'"
[Mark 9v38-49 The Message]

"Salt is good for seasoning. But if it loses its flavour, how do
you make it salty again? You must have the qualities of salt
among yourselves and live in peace with each other."
[Mark 9v50 NLT]

He began to speak…

Weighty Words,
Brined right through and stinging to the core.
To preserve.

Salted words,
Reaching deep into the flesh wound of shared humanity.
To heal.

Seasoned words,
Bringing flavours of heaven to earth.
To transform.

For the smallest grains of value, of honour, of a heart towards God,
Become a catalyst for turning bland living
Into the taste of real
Life.

So who is Jesus?

Jesus is the speaker of salty words.

Something to consider

Jesus was was never a hypocrite, and lived what He taught to the core. He was the one who could speak salty words with deep love, and deep truth. In cooking, it is the small things, like tiny granules of salt, which determine the flavour of the whole dish. In our lives, maybe it's the same. Maybe it is the little things that make all the difference. Little things, which turn out to be big things, like value, like honour, like a heart turned towards God.

Maybe it's those things that truly make us salty, so we can bring out the God flavours in the earth. So we can preserve all that is good, and be bringers of peace.

Something to pray

Jesus, thank you that when you speak salty words, they are spoken with love and truth. I find that I often fall so short of your salty words. I'm sorry for when I lose my saltiness. Thank you that your grace covers and re-flavours my whole life. Please fill all the little things of my heart with the flavour of you, so I can help the stuff around me taste a bit more like peace, a bit more like life, a bit more like love. Amen.

day 46
painted into one

"Pharisees came up, intending to give [Jesus] a hard time. They asked, 'Is it legal for a man to divorce his wife?' Jesus said, 'What did Moses command?' They answered, 'Moses gave permission to fill out a certificate of dismissal and divorce her.' Jesus said, 'Moses wrote this command only as a concession to your hardhearted ways. In the original creation, God made male and female to be together. Because of this, a man leaves father and mother, and in marriage he becomes one flesh with a woman—no longer two individuals, but forming a new unity. Because God created this organic union of the two sexes, no one should desecrate his art by cutting them apart.'" [Mark 10v1-12 The Message]

The crowds gathered close and the religious one edged nearer, trying to make Him stumble over words, trying to trip Him over the letter of the law. But He saw clearer than they ever had And so He began to paint a picture of that which they could not see.
A picture of the beginning:

Where the Maker had designed hearts in union and lives entwined in the loving, and the living, and the delighting in each other.

This original art of lives painted into one. Like He is One.

Where the lines of distinction blur,
Where separation stops,
And where every heart
Is held in the holding.

For He had never wanted
Hearts to be
Torn.

So who is Jesus?

Jesus is the one who reminds us of love.

Something to consider

In life, hearts are often torn and brokenness is very real. Sometimes through our own choices, sometimes through the choices of others, and sometimes through a mixture of both. However God always longs to heal and restore all the broken parts of our lives. He delights in giving us a new start, and He always meets us with love.

The Pharisees however, were so caught up with the letter of the law that they often missed the heartbeat of God. Jesus seemed to cut through their judgment, and redefine what the law actually was: to love God and to love people.

To hold carefully the heart of another and not easily discard something so precious.

Jesus never comes to bring shame, but to bring the love and the grace of God, for whatever the story of life has been. He also reminds us of the desire of the Father for hearts to love and to be loved, within His greater love.

Maybe, today we can place value on the people around us, whatever their relationship is to us. Because, it is always the desire of God for people to know real love.

Something to pray

Jesus, thank you that you are the healer of the broken hearted. Where areas of my life have been torn, you come with grace to heal. Please help me value the people in my world, whatever their relationship is to me. May I not treat another person lightly but place worth on them, because I know that you do too. Amen.

day 47

learning from
the little

"One day some parents brought their children to Jesus
so he could touch and bless them … He said to them,
'Let the children come to me. Don't stop them! For the
Kingdom of God belongs to those who are like these
children. I tell you the truth, anyone who doesn't receive
the Kingdom of God like a child will never enter it.' Then
he took the children in his arms and placed his hands on
their heads and blessed them."
[Mark 10v13-16 NLT]

The taller ones frowned. They did not like the tiresome interruption of small things. They were more accustomed to the ways of the world, the ways of stature, the ways of man. They knew how life should go and would stick to the schedule of first and last.

But the little ones didn't care for such things.

These ones with tangled hair, scuffed knees, and eyes wide with wonder.

These ones who smiled a thousand dimples, gasping at the world anew, Breathing in endless days of whimsy and daydream.

These ones who ran, and danced, and skipped, and hopped, and sat, and stood, and played, and stared at the mystery.

These ones did not care for the costumed pride and parade. And neither did He.

This carpenter turned preacher man. This one with the dusty feet, and the wider than wide heart, and the fuller than full dream of a happy ever after. This one who would cut through life's tangled tree just to reach the smallest. Just to scoop them in His arms. Just to lift the little and smile a thousand dimples on Each one.

So who is Jesus?

Jesus is the one who welcomes us into wide-eyed wonder.

Something to consider

The children came to Jesus just as they were. They had no concept of importance or busyness. They had no pretence and no entitlement. They came to Him in simple trust and wide-eyed wonder. And they were so very welcome.

But how often do we get too old in our thinking? Too tainted in trust? Too disillusioned in delight? I wonder if we have we become too tall?

Maybe it's time to learn from the little. To rediscover simple trust. To see with wide-eyed wonder. Maybe it's time to splash in some puddles with Jesus again!

Something to pray

Beautiful Jesus, I love it that you welcome me deep into simple trust and wide- eyed wonder. Help me never get too tall!

I want to always be one who comes to you without pretence, and in the deepest delight of you. Help me learn from the little, and then maybe I will see a bit more the magnitude of you. Amen.

day 48
treasure seekers

"'Good Teacher, what must I do to get eternal life?' ... Jesus looked him hard in the eye—and loved him! He said, 'There's one thing left: Go sell whatever you own and give it to the poor. All your wealth will then be heavenly wealth. And come follow me.' ... he walked off with a heavy heart. He was holding on tight to a lot of things, and not about to let go ... Jesus said, 'Do you have any idea how difficult it is for people who "have it all" to enter God's kingdom? ...I'd say it is easier for a camel to go through a needle's eye...' Then who has any chance at all?' they asked. Jesus was blunt: 'No chance at all if you think you can pull it off by yourself. Every chance in the world if you let God do it.'"
[Mark 10v17-31 The Message]

He was one of the treasure seekers.

One filled with that aching desire
To behold. To taste. To see
The essence that fuels living and breathing.

Sometimes a glimpse was gained, carried on the wind, carried on a prayer.
And he breathed it in, afraid to breathe out, in case the moment shattered.

He held his breath, and held on tight to all the glimmers of treasure he could own.

And then came the Windswept One. The One brushed with eternal days.

Inviting him deep into the mystery of letting go, of abandoning all, of stepping through the needle's eye and stepping into the taste and the see of True treasure

Worth everything.

Here he could breathe it in, breathe out,
And breathe in again.

So who is Jesus?

Jesus is true treasure.

Something to consider

The man's heart was entangled in all that he could do, all that he could prove, and all that he could own. But Jesus invited him to let go the 'all of himself', and to embrace the all of God. The sad thing about this story is that the man, who so ached for the things of eternity, did not realise the treasure he was being offered. He chose the all of himself, and never discovered the all of God. He never discovered the treasure that his heart really longed for.

It makes me wonder if I'm holding on too tightly to the 'all of me', and to what I think is treasure. Whereas the path to true treasure is in trusting my all to the all of God.

Something to pray

Precious Jesus, you are my heart's true treasure. You are the one I desire. I'm sorry for when I cling so tightly to the 'all of me'. Please help me walk through the needle's eye, where unbelief is lost and I find faith. Where the storehouses of all I've sought are found within your gaze. And where the mystery of everything is glimpsed, then fades away, in the light of you. Amen.

day 49
certain and sure

"Taking the twelve disciples aside, Jesus once more began to describe everything that was about to happen to him. 'Listen,' he said, 'we're going up to Jerusalem, where the Son of Man will be betrayed to the leading priests and the teachers of religious law. They will sentence him to die and hand him over to the Romans. They will mock him, spit on him, flog him with a whip, and kill him, but after three days he will rise again.'"
[Mark 10v32-34 NLT]

He spoke of things to come, and they
trembled at the unknown.
It was a path they did not want to take.
Thick with fog.

Confusion settled heavy,
and the way through was cloud dense
in dread.

Hope was turning murky,
and each breath was daunted.

But the one from ancient days spoke of
things to come.
Through the shrouded haze, to all that
was
Certain and Sure.

Like He was
Certain and Sure.

Like He would always be
Certain and Sure.

So in the shaking, those after

Could stand.

So who is Jesus?

Jesus is Certain and Sure.

Something to consider

The disciples had no clue as to how
the story would end. They just found
themselves, like we often do, facing
the unknown. That place when
everything becomes shaky ground
and we tremble at what lies ahead.

But Jesus always knew how the story
would finish. He knew that God would
make the way.

In our shaking times, let's cling to
Jesus who forever remains Certain
and Sure.
He holds the story of our lives, and the
story isn't over yet.

Something to pray

My Jesus, thank you that you are
Certain and Sure. In all the shakiness
of my life, you are steadfast. You are
the one who knows the path through,
so I'm clinging tightly to you. Thank
you that the story isn't over yet. Thank
you that you are making the way.
Amen.

day 50
love
poured out

"James and John, Zebedee's sons, came up to him. 'Teacher …
Arrange it,' they said, 'so that we will be awarded the highest
places of honour in your glory...' When the other ten heard
of this conversation, they lost their tempers with James and
John. Jesus got them together to settle things down. 'You've
observed how godless rulers throw their weight around … It's
not going to be that way with you. Whoever wants to be great
must become a servant. Whoever wants to be first among you
must be your slave. That is what the Son of Man has done: He
came to serve, not to be served—and then to give away his life
in exchange for many who are held hostage.'"
[Mark 10v35-45 The Message]

The holy one pulled down the pomp and the pride, and then would smash it against the beams of a wooden cross.

Nailing the message loud and clear…

Greatness is to pour out.

Like blood poured out, like love poured out, like the thorns pushed in and a heart wrenched over the soil of us all.

And he would hang on the beams of that wooden cross, to lift us earthen ones from the dirt.

Calling the once upon a fisherlads, and all else who would follow, into real greatness.

Where we cast our manmade crowns before him and stamp foolish pride into the dust.

Our lives, like clay, moulded into art. To display Him.

Our art, fashioned into worship. To honour Him.

Our worship, formed in the heart. Because we love Him.

Because He first loved us.

So who is Jesus?

Jesus is truly great.

Something to consider

Jesus lived what He taught to the full, not for a show, but because that was who He was. He was love and so He poured out love. He poured out everything for us.

How great the love He has completely and utterly lavished on us!!!!

Let's gaze again at Jesus, the one who gave everything. And then, when we are filled with His love, it cannot help but pour out from us in love for others.

Something to pray

My Jesus, you are stunning in your sacrifice. I cannot take it in that you loved me that much. May your love so fill me that it then flows out of me to others. Help me see clearly what really matters in life and in love. Help me be a bit more like you, not because of a show, but because it is more who I am becoming. Amen.

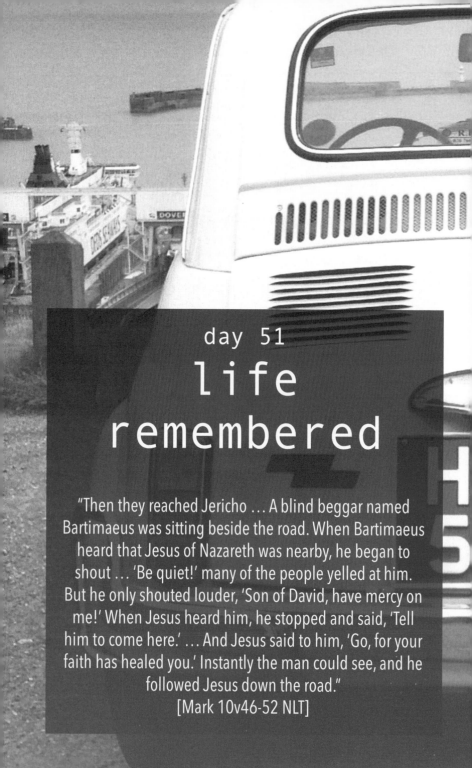

day 51
life
remembered

"Then they reached Jericho ... A blind beggar named Bartimaeus was sitting beside the road. When Bartimaeus heard that Jesus of Nazareth was nearby, he began to shout ... 'Be quiet!' many of the people yelled at him. But he only shouted louder, 'Son of David, have mercy on me!' When Jesus heard him, he stopped and said, 'Tell him to come here.' ... And Jesus said to him, 'Go, for your faith has healed you.' Instantly the man could see, and he followed Jesus down the road."
[Mark 10v46-52 NLT]

Feet paced past, marking the moments with the always ending of NO.

Halting him in the days, turning to weeks, turning to months, turning to A life forgot.

Depending on the kindness of a stranger, hoping for the mercy of a friend.

Then the God man came by. And life held in the stop dared to believe above, to rise above, to shout above the noise, and the distain, and the never ending NO.

For this God man would hear the C R Y.

And He did. And He marked the moment with His sight bursting, colour blasting, light erupting YES. Marking the begin again of a life remembered.

In the kindness of a stranger, in the mercy of a friend.

So who is Jesus?

Jesus is the one who hears the cry.

Something to consider

Bartimaeus was surround by the constant 'No' of circumstances, yet he believed that Jesus was his answer. And so, even though people didn't really shout at rabbis, Bartimaeus cried out and then kept crying out.

I wonder if, in the persistence of the cry, faith was being forged. And maybe it was that faith forged which released the miracle. Because you only cry out so persistently if you begin to believe that your cry will be heard. If you begin to be convinced that there will be a response. If you begin to have an undeterred confidence in the one whom you are crying out to. Maybe in the persistence of the cry, you begin to be sure that mercy will be shown, otherwise you would give up.

So, Bartimaeus cried out, just one more time. And Jesus heard the cry. Because Jesus always hears the cry.

Maybe it's time to cry out just one more time for the promises of God, one more time for the miracles of God, one more time for the kingdom of God to come in your life.

For your cry stops Jesus in his tracks.

Something to pray

My Jesus, thank you that you always hear the cry. For the 'No's of my life, I cry out to you, and I cry out again. For I am beginning to be convinced that you hear, that you answer, that you are for me, that you can do anything, that your promises are true, that you love me, that you want to bless me, that you are enough for me.
I am convinced that you are good and will do good, and that you always hear my cry. Amen.

day 52
there comes
a time

"...Then they brought the colt to Jesus and threw their
garments over it, and he sat on it ... Many in the crowd
spread their garments on the road ahead of him, and
others spread leafy branches they had cut in the fields.
Jesus was in the center of the procession, and the people
all around him were shouting, 'Praise God! Blessings on
the one who comes in the name of the Lord! Blessings on
the coming Kingdom of our ancestor David! Praise God in
highest heaven!'"
[Mark 11v1-11 NLT]

Expectancy shook every weary space
And the times were on tiptoe,
Straining to see

The long awaited one.

For into centuries of hoping,
The end game had begun.

Entering on a donkey,
Clothed in grace-soaked robes,
Paving the path for Kingdom here,
Kingdom now, Kingdom come.

Soon oppression's claim would be displaced.
And the streets could not contain the Jubilation,

While darkness trembled at the dance and the shout

of Liberation.

So who is Jesus?

Jesus is the long-awaited one.

Something to consider

There comes a time when it is time.
It is time for the promises of God to come in fullness, it is time for God's light to break in, it is time for God's life to reign. And when it's time, nothing can contain it, squash it, or steal it.

People had been waiting for the Messiah for centuries, and it often must have seemed like the promise was not going to be fulfilled. It often must have seemed like God had forgotten.

But God does not forget his word. He knows the time, and he knows the way the word finds its fulfillment. Even if it looks unusual, riding on a donkey.

Don't give up. Don't give up. Don't give up.

There will come a time.

Something to pray

My Jesus, thank you that you were the fulfillment of promises from down the centuries. Your coming testified to the faithfulness of the Father. Your arriving silenced every voice that said God would not do what He had said. Thank you that you know the time, and that you make everything beautiful in its time.

Thank you that there will come a time for all that you have said for my life.

I trust in you and join the jubilation of liberation. For my hope is in you, the long awaited one. Amen.

day 53
ripe
with life

"As they left Bethany the next day, he was hungry. Off in the distance he saw a fig tree in full leaf. He came up to it expecting to find something for breakfast, but found nothing but fig leaves. (It wasn't yet the season for figs.) He addressed the tree: 'No one is going to eat fruit from you again–ever!' And his disciples overheard him."
[Mark 11v12-14 The Message]

It was a full leafed, lush leaved, lavish
leaved
Boast of fruitfulness.

Promising much.
Holding little.

Stuck in the thinness of pretense,
Where appearance imitates substance,
And façade conceals emptiness.

He was not impressed.

This One
Ripe with life and
Full of truth.

He had no time for such a show.

So who is Jesus?

Jesus is full of truth.

Something to consider

The fig tree looked impressive. The fig
tree was boasting of fruit, for fig trees
only present full leaf when the fruit
is there to be eaten. But when Jesus
looked closer, there were no figs!

Now, I don't think that Jesus hated
trees, so maybe Jesus is commenting
on things with an impressive outward
appearance but with no actual
substance.

And it makes me ask myself, are there
any areas of my worship of God, my
walk with God, or of my life, where
it has become more about the show
rather than the substance? For I want
my life to be filled with things that are
true, worship that is true, a heart that
is true. Then fruit will be the natural
produce of my life, and then I will be
more like Jesus, who is full of life and
truth.

Something to pray

My Jesus, may my life not be a grand
appearance of all that is fruitful and
good, but with no substance to it. May
my life, and walk with you, be true in
the core. Please help me live full of
your life and truth. Amen.

day 54
out of the shadows

"Immediately on entering the Temple Jesus started throwing out everyone who had set up shop there, buying and selling … 'My house was designated a house of prayer for the nations; You've turned it into a hangout for thieves...' At evening, Jesus and his disciples left the city. In the morning, walking along the road, they saw the fig tree, shriveled to a dry stick … Jesus was matter-of-fact: 'Embrace this God-life. Really embrace it, and nothing will be too much for you. This mountain, for instance: Just say, "Go jump in the lake"–no shuffling or shilly-shallying– and it's as good as done. That's why I urge you to pray for absolutely everything, ranging from small to large. Include everything as you embrace this God-life, and you'll get God's everything.'"
[Mark 11v15-25 The Message]

He began to call things out.
Out of the distort, out of the show,
Out of the shadows
Of what it had all become,
And back to the beginning.

Where the Author had dreamed to life
His story of love soaked earth.
Breathed warm to life
Our story of hearts' true home.

Where heaven's kiss rests,
And we are held in the
Forever embrace.

For there the shadows flee,
And all things become possible,

Just like at the beginning.

So who is Jesus?

Jesus is the one who calls us out of the shadows.

Something to consider

The temple represented a place of encounter. Where people could come close, and closer still, to the Holy God. But everything had become so distorted. Religion had suffocated faith, and what was designed beautiful had been made ugly with greed, pretense, hard hearts, and the total sham of it all.

God never wanted that for humanity. For God's story had always been about relationship, built in the fullness of His love. The polluted temple and the fruitless fig tree, show us how false everything had become. And Jesus was angry at the distortion.

Jesus calls us out of all such shadows. Back to what it is all really about. Where we walk in intimacy with God. Where His life infuses everything. Where heaven kisses earth. And in that place, all things become possible.

Something to pray

Beautiful Jesus, thank you that you love me enough not to leave me in the shadows. Thank you that you beckon me back to heart encounter with you, to intimacy with you, to my heart's true home. Thank you that in that place, heaven is opened wide and all things become possible. I want to live my days in your forever embrace. Amen.

day 55
gifts of grace

"…as they were walking through the Temple, the high priests, religion scholars, and leaders came up and demanded, 'Show us your credentials. Who authorized you to speak and act like this?' Jesus responded, 'First let me ask you a question. Answer my question and then I'll present my credentials. About the baptism of John–who authorized it: heaven or humans? Tell me.' They were on the spot, and knew it … 'We don't know,' they said. Jesus replied, 'Then I won't answer your question either.'"
[Mark 11v27-33 The Message]

He was treading on their turf.

This once upon a carpenter from the edge of nowhere.

Bold in His walk. Audacious in His host of Heavenly claims.

He was not one of them.

Yet He was striding their streets, stepping over their terrain.

Walking right past their self-inflated rank.

The people were hungry for Him.
Eager for the words
Oh so sweet with life,
Oh so rich in gifts of grace.

And they did not like it.

But He did not need their authorisation,
For He was from Ancient of Days,
And the very ground beneath their feet

Testified His Name.

So who is Jesus?

Jesus is God's gift of grace.

Something to consider

The religious leaders were so captivated by their own right standing, their own control, their own understanding, that they completely missed God's gift of grace to them. They were waiting for the Messiah, the one to come with authority and God's reign. However, even though He was walking their very streets, they did not recognize Him.

Maybe, because it looked different to how they had thought. Maybe, because it disrupted the status quo. Or maybe just because it was so audacious in grace that they could not accept it.

May we not be so full of our own understanding, that we miss seeing the gift of God that could be right in front of us.

Something to pray

My Jesus, thank you for your gifts of grace that are waiting to be discovered, on every path I tread. Help me not be so fixed in my agenda, that I don't recognise the things of you. Help me be humble enough to see the gift of you even on well-worn turf, even in the things I don't understand, even in the things which look different to how I had thought. Help me have my eyes wide open for your gifts of grace. Amen.

stories unfolding

"A man planted a vineyard … turned it over to the farmhands, and went off on a trip. At the time for harvest, he sent a servant back to the farmhands to collect his profits. They grabbed him, beat him up, and sent him off empty-handed … And on and on, many others … Finally there was only one left: a beloved son … They grabbed him, killed him, and threw him over the fence. What do you think the owner of the vineyard will do? Right. He'll come and clean house. Then he'll assign the care of the vineyard to others. Read it for yourselves in Scripture: That stone the masons threw out is now the cornerstone!"
[Mark 12v1-12 The Message]

[And so the writer of stories, began to tell a tale of trust torn]

For once, a gift was given with trust to care, trust to cherish, trust to tend,
All that was precious to the Maker.

But the ways of man entered the twist and the turn,
Spiralling hearts all the way down to hit the pit of
Entitled Greed.

The clod of soiled trust compounded,
Pushing heavy on the shoulders of
The Maker's Son,
As they rejected and scorned this Rightful One.

And Trust was Torn.

[The listeners leaned in. Some intrigued. Some exposed. But the writer of stories was not yet done…]

But when sorrow poured out, love poured down,
To wash away the dirt and filth of soiled earth.
Revealing the capstone, the cornerstone, the centre rock, the solid rock,
the Rightful One, the Glorious Son, the Now and Always

True Foundation.

So who is Jesus?

Jesus is the True Foundation.

Something to consider

Jesus was telling this story directly against the religious leaders. Those who had been trusted with the most precious thing of all, God's word and God's people. But they had become entitled, and broken trust with their Maker. They had rejected Him so much, that they would end up killing His Son.

But the one they rejected, was actually the Maker's cornerstone.
The eternal foundation. The capstone on which everything stands.

In whatever you face today, please know that Jesus is the cornerstone. He is strong enough for you. On Him, you can stand.

Something to pray

My Jesus, thank you that you are the cornerstone. You are the solid rock. You are my true foundation. You are strong enough for me. And I gratefully stand on all that you are today. Amen.

day 57

tangled webs

"Later the leaders sent some Pharisees and supporters
of Herod to trap Jesus into saying something for which
he could be arrested. 'Teacher,' they said, 'we know how
honest you are ... Now tell us—is it right to pay taxes to
Caesar or not? Should we pay them, or shouldn't we?'
Jesus saw through their hypocrisy and said, 'Why are you
trying to trap me? Show me a Roman coin, and I'll tell you
... give to Caesar what belongs to Caesar, and give to God
what belongs to God.'"
[Mark 12v13-17 NLT]

They tried, once again, to spin a trap.

These ones so stuck in the struggle,
Caught in the Strive,
Ensnared in the own and the Disown,
The hold and the Withhold,
Entangled in their knotted web of
the Prove and the Self-Preserve.

But He would not be dawn into their
spidery net,

For freedom cuts through all throttling
threads,

Releasing the heart

to soar
in the High Places of

HONOUR.

Jesus is the one who calls us to the
high places.

The religious leaders asked Jesus
one of the most loaded questions in
Israel at that time. For the people of
Israel were subject to the Romans,
and desperately wanted freedom from
their taxes and power. However, to not
pay taxes would be a massive defiance
of Roman rule. If Jesus answered
yes or no, it would be seen as either
rebellion or revolution from whichever
side you stood.

However, Jesus calls them, and us, to
see higher things. He calls us to the
high places of honour.

For in His grace we don't need to cling
to our self-proving, we don't need
to live in the withhold, we are free to
give freely. In His grace we are free to
esteem, to praise, to exalt, to value,
and to place value upon. In His grace
we are free to honour our God, the
one who is worthy of ALL honour. In
His grace we also find ourselves free
enough to honour others. For in His
grace, there is nothing to fear.

And it makes me wonder how can I
honour God and others in my world,
with a little less self-preservation and
a little more heart abandon.

Beautiful Jesus, you are worthy of my
deepest devotion and honour. You are
worthy of every accolade and every
bit of esteem that I possibly imagine.
Thank you that you call me to be free
enough in you to be able to bring
honour to you, and also to be able to
honour others. Pease help me live with
a little less self-preservation and a little
more heart abandon. Help me live in
the freedom of honour. Amen.

one day when

"Some Sadducees, the party that denies any possibility of
resurrection, came up and asked, 'Teacher, Moses wrote that if a
man dies and leaves a wife but no child, his brother is obligated to
marry the widow and have children. Well, there once were seven
brothers… ' Jesus said, 'You're way off base … you don't know how
God works. After the dead are raised up … all our ecstasies and
intimacies then will be with God. And regarding the dead, whether
or not they are raised, don't you ever read the Bible? How God at
the bush said to Moses, "I am—not was—the God of Abraham, the
God of Isaac, and the God of Jacob"? The living God is God of the
living, not the dead. You're way, way off base.'"
[Mark 12 v18-27 The Message]

He began to give them a glimpse of the One Day When.

For now, the longing of the heart echoes deep,
Ringing through every hollow place with the ache of the ages.

For now, we see the spaces between Here and There,
And gaze across the Reach
Feeling the Separation.

Our hearts held in the always Yearning
For the One Day…

When we are breathed warm to life in the unveiling,
When we awake warm to love in the appearing,
When we are held warm to touch in His returning.

That One Day when separation stops and our hearts are forever found

In Life.
In Him.

So who is Jesus?

Jesus is Life for us Now, and Then.

Something to consider

The Sadducees wanted to debate whether there was life after death, whether there would be a resurrection. Jesus clearly states that God is the God of Life. He always has been, and always will be. He is the bringer of life now and for eternity.

Jesus then takes the debate one step further, to help us see a glimpse of eternity. When even the deepest intimacy of earth will fade into the shallows, compared to the depths of being loved in God.

There is great hope Now, for the God of all life is with us Now. He is the God of Abraham, of Isaac, of Jacob, of you and of me. We are found and loved by Him, Now.
And there is great hope Then, for we will be forever found, and forever loved by Him, for eternity.
He is with us Now, and Then.

Something to pray

Beautiful Jesus, thank you that in you I am forever found. Thank you that you are the God of life for me in the now, and you are the God of life for me in the then. Help me know I am forever held in your love. Amen.

day 59

pulsing true

"One of the religion scholars came up ... 'Which is most
important of all the commandments?'
Jesus said, 'The first in importance is, "...love the Lord
God with all your passion and prayer and intelligence and
energy." And here is the second: "Love others as well as
you love yourself."
... The religion scholar said, 'A wonderful answer, Teacher!
So lucid and accurate—that God is one and there is no
other. And loving him with all passion and intelligence
and energy, and loving others as well as you love yourself.
Why, that's better than all offerings and sacrifices put
together!'
When Jesus realized how insightful he was, he said,
'You're almost there, right on the border of God's
kingdom.'"
[Mark 12 V28-34 The Message]

One of the searching drew close.

Inclining his ear to hear the swelling sound,
Like a thousand heartbeats pulsing through the centuries
Of living and breathing and hoping, now nearing,

Charged full of Love Divine.

The rhythm began, way back then
In love, through love, for love,
Pulsing true, pulsing strong, His love.

Ever surrounding, now nearing,
Inviting the searching to hear the sound,
Which heralds the kiss to life.

In love, through love, for love,
Pulsing true, pulsing strong,
Ever surrounding, now nearing,

Charged full of Love Divine.

So who is Jesus?

Jesus is Love Divine.

Something to consider

It has always been about love.
From the very beginning we were breathed to life, kissed to life, in love. We were authored in love. The purpose of it all was to live in His love, and to live in His love for each other.

And yet we seem to have forgotten.

But Jesus beckons us to remember, to hear the heartbeat of Love Divine and to truly live in love. With God, and with others.

Something to pray

My Jesus, thank you that you breathe me to life in your love. Please help me to live fully alive in your Love Divine. I want my heartbeat to be pulsing love for you, and for others. Amen.

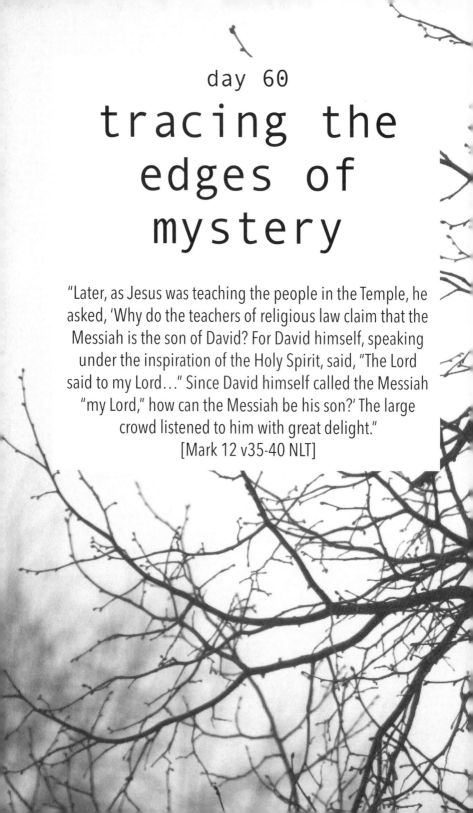

tracing the edges of mystery

"Later, as Jesus was teaching the people in the Temple, he asked, 'Why do the teachers of religious law claim that the Messiah is the son of David? For David himself, speaking under the inspiration of the Holy Spirit, said, "The Lord said to my Lord…" Since David himself called the Messiah "my Lord," how can the Messiah be his son?' The large crowd listened to him with great delight."
[Mark 12 v35-40 NLT]

He began to trace the edges of mystery,
Drawing lines forwards and back,
With the ink of grace that outspans the age.

And the world held its breath with the whisper of "Messiah".
Our God will save.

He traced the edges to way back when,
Causing hearts to wonder at The Wonderful, The Counsellor,
Like the mother had wondered at her sleeping babe.

And the world held its breath with the whisper of "Messiah".
Our God will save.

And He traced the lines through longing time,
Through the earth so torn, and lives misaligned,
Still he traced the lines drawn thick with grace
Of The King Who Was, The King Always.

And the world held its breath,
With His whisper
With His name

Messiah. Our God Will Save.

So who is Jesus?

Jesus is Messiah.

Something to consider

When Jesus spoke of the Messiah, He spoke of Himself. He spoke of God's saving grace, and He spoke of deep mystery. For He was the one who was from before time, and who outspans every age.

Into all the hopes and dreams of the years, into life so torn, Jesus came as Messiah. Our God will save.

Jesus still is Messiah. Our God will save.

So, maybe into the depths of what you are facing today, you could whisper those grace-staggering, life-staggering words: 'Messiah, my God will save'.

Something to pray

Beautiful Jesus, thank you that you are the one who was, and who is, and who is to come. I whisper your name today into the longing of the years. I whisper your name today into the impossibilities. I whisper your name today in hope and expectancy. Messiah, My God will save. Amen.

Space to Breathe...

day 61
devoted

"Sitting across from the offering box, he was observing how the crowd tossed money in for the collection. Many of the rich were making large contributions. One poor widow came up and put in two small coins–a measly two cents. Jesus called his disciples over and said, 'The truth is that this poor widow gave more to the collection than all the others put together. All the others gave what they'll never miss; she gave extravagantly what she couldn't afford–she gave her all.'"
[Mark 12v41-44 The Message]

Everything was in the hustle and bustle of flaunt and prove,
As the coins chinked together in a clattering of spectacle.
Hard-edged in the gold clang of have and own, make and do,
With life set in the cold clank of Duty Embossed Reputation.

And then she came along. Lowly. Humbled in the years.

Just one poor widow. Just one of many. Just one getting by
In the unseen, unknown, unnumbered days.
Her life pressed through with sorrow and devotion.

Quietly she brought her gift. It was an offering costly.

And to Him, the one from Ancient of Days, it held weight
More than all the empty clamour.
For she was one who had lost much.
She was one who gave much.
She was one Devoted.

And He saw. And He knew. And He loved.

So who is Jesus?

Jesus is the one who knows.

Something to consider

Sometimes it's in the small things, that the deep things are revealed.

To everyone else this woman's life was forgotten, discarded, and not blessed by God. She was poor. She was a widow. She was one of the least.
They went about making a show of their worship, but she really knew what it meant to worship. To bring that gift of trust and devotion, even with the small things, and even in the hard places. Her gift was noticed by heaven.

And sometimes it costs everything. Whether worship is offering a prayer of praise in unnumbered days, a giving of what is precious, an act of obedience just because He's asked, a choice to trust even through sorrows hour. It's those gifts of the moments, those 'small' things that cost so much. It's those things, which are precious in the eyes of the Saviour.

Please take courage again today: Jesus sees, He knows. He loves.

Something to pray

My Jesus, thank you that you know. You know all the unseen things. And in the small moments, and in the costly moments, may you find in me a heart of devotion. Because I love you, because you first loved me. Thank you that you know. Amen.

keep looking up

"Now learn a lesson from the fig tree. When its branches bud … you know that summer is near. In the same way, when you see all these things taking place, you can know that his return is very near, right at the door. I tell you the truth, this generation will not pass from the scene before all these things take place. Heaven and earth will disappear, but my words will never disappear."
[Mark 13v1-31 NLT]

And the earth groans.

Through the tearing, and the breaking,
and the whirling of anguish lived
Over and over again.
Through humanity ripped by hate, rent
in loss, and dashed to the core.

Through all the shadow hours the
earth groans,
Just like hearts groan under the
weight of it all.

Yet, a day is coming.

And the earth is always turning,
curving through the centuries,
Spinning in the longing and the
looking for the new day dawning,
Hoping for the one day approaching
when sorrow will still,
And the King will return.

So lift up your eyes!
See through the spinning, look to the
appearing,
There is an anchor steady though the
grieving,
Face forwards in the watching, in the
waiting, in the hoping,

For a day is coming.

The day of His return.

So who is Jesus?

Jesus is the King who will return.

Something to consider

Sometimes we feel the weight of the
earth's groaning more than at other
times. Sometimes we feel the shadow
hours thick on our skin.

In those times, know again that there
is coming a day when He will return.
When torn earth will be remade, and a
new day will begin.

And in the midst of the spinning,
may we know that our God is with us.
His word is an anchor that will never
fail. His love is the constant in all the
turmoil of our broken earth. He is close
to us. And He is coming. The story
doesn't stop here. The story finds its
proper end in Him.

Something to pray

Jesus, sometimes it's all I can do to
whisper your name when I see the
sorrow of the earth, when I feel the
sorrow within. But I look to you, I watch
for you, I wait for you. I know a day is
coming when you will return. And I
know that here and now you are with
us, you are close to us, and you are in
the midst of it all. Amen.

day 63
light hope
ready

"But the exact day and hour? No one knows that, not even heaven's angels, not even the Son. Only the Father. So keep a sharp lookout, for you don't know the timetable. It's like a man who takes a trip, leaving home and putting his servants in charge ... So, stay at your post, watching. You have no idea when the homeowner is returning ... Stay at your post. Keep watch."
[Mark 13v32-37 The Message]

Can you feel it?
The earth is tiptoe waiting,
Anticipating the Homecoming.

Into the dark there is this glimmer,
Brimming over the edge of all the
sorrow,
With its warming, welcoming

Light.

A glimmer of hope igniting. A glimmer
of love uncurling.
A glimmer of life returning, in the
arms open wide of Homecoming.

And there is this beckoning, this
longing, this calling, this responding.

So light courage ready,
Light hope ready,
Join the tiptoe waiting,
Anticipate the warming,
Welcoming
Light

Of Homecoming.

So who is Jesus?

Jesus is our Homecoming.

Something to consider

Sometimes it takes courage to keep
on hoping, when all we see are the
shadows. But into the dark, there is a
light. His light.

And there is the beacon of
Homecoming. When He will return,
and we will forever be found in Him –
our hearts' true home.

Maybe into the shadowy places of our
here and now, it's time to light courage
ready, to light hope ready. For there is
a light.

And there will be a Homecoming.

Something to pray

Beautiful Jesus, thank you that you are
light in my darkness. Thank you that
one day, there will be a homecoming.
I'm lighting courage ready. I'm lighting
hope ready. I'm joining the watching
and the waiting. Thank you that you
are with me. Thank you that you are my
homecoming. Amen.

day 64

the beauty
of abandon

"Meanwhile, Jesus was in Bethany ... While he was eating, a woman came in with a beautiful alabaster jar of expensive perfume made from essence of nard. She broke open the jar and poured the perfume over his head.
Some of those at the table were indignant. 'Why waste such expensive perfume?' ... But Jesus replied, 'Leave her alone ... She has done what she could and has anointed my body for burial ahead of time. I tell you the truth, wherever the Good News is preached throughout the world, this woman's deed will be remembered and discussed.'"
[Mark 14v1-11 NLT]

She knew she shouldn't be there.
It was against the tide of how things should go,
But still she entered. Eyes only on Him:

This once upon a carpenter, this One who held her heart.

They were indignant, but she pressed through.
And in the breaking, and the pouring, and the surrender of extravagant love,
She gave her all.
[Like He would soon give His all.]

The perfumed essence of her offering filled every tender space,
And He was bathed in oceans of costly love,

Anointed in the beauty of abandon.

The others despised such a gift,
But He saw her worth:

This One who held her heart.

So who is Jesus?

Jesus is the one who sees our worth.

Something to consider

This woman was courageous enough to love, and to pour devotion out. Even though it was against all social norms and even though it was costly.

She did not realise she was anointing Jesus for burial. She did not realise the weight of the offering she brought. But Jesus did and He valued it.

I wonder how often we hold back from being abandoned in our devotion, because of fear? Maybe we can learn from this woman who loved Jesus enough, to give her all. For such an offering of worship, of costly love, is never wasted on Him. Such a gift is valued by the One who sees our worth and who holds our hearts.

Something to pray

Beautiful Jesus, thank you that you love me with costly love. You poured out your all for me. Thank you that you always hold my heart with worth and tenderness. My Jesus, you are worth everything, so I pour out my love for you in the beauty of abandon. Amen.

day 65

a chair
pulled up

"...As they were eating, Jesus took some bread and blessed it. Then he broke it in pieces and gave it to the disciples, saying, 'Take it, for this is my body.'
And he took a cup of wine and gave thanks to God for it. He gave it to them, and they all drank from it. And he said to them, 'This is my blood, which confirms the covenant between God and his people. It is poured out as a sacrifice for many.'"
[Mark 14v12-26 NLT]

And so a table was set, with a chair pulled up for each one.

For each one so covered in the dust of the earth,
For each one who would betray, and deny,
And push the tearing wounds
So deep.

He knew it was time. He knew what was to come.

And so He beckoned them to the feast.

And there at His table,
The unworthy were welcomed
To taste grace found in the ripping,
To savor mercy found in the pouring,
To receive redemption found in His giving.

The table was set

In brokenness and healing.

With a chair pulled up for each one.

So who is Jesus?

Jesus is the one who pulls up a chair for us.

Something to consider

Jesus knew He was going to the cross, and so He invited those He loved to a feast. A feast of closeness. A feast to show the way.

They might not have fully understood the significance of that Passover feast, but they would understand it more in the days to come. They would see how His blood would be enough for how they would fail. They would see that His wounds would be enough for the healing of each one.

Whatever we are facing, Jesus pulls up a chair for us at His table of grace. Taste of Him. Savor Him. Receive redemption's feast again.

Something to pray

My Jesus, I cannot even begin to understand what you were willing to go through for me.

Thank you that you invite me to the feast of grace poured out, of mercy poured in, and of redemption wide enough for us all.

Thank you that you pull up a chair for me. I am so grateful I get to sit at your feast. Amen.

through & beyond

"Jesus told them, 'You're all going to feel that your world is falling apart and that it's my fault ... But after I am raised up, I will go ahead of you, leading the way to Galilee.' Peter blurted out, 'Even if everyone else is ashamed of you when things fall to pieces, I won't be.' Jesus said, 'Don't be so sure. Today, this very night in fact, before the rooster crows twice, you will deny me three times.'"
[Mark 14v27-31 The Message]

And so the shadows began to settle.

Curling around the edges of that which
had been cherished,
Tainting the treasured with leaden
shades,
Turning the day into those night-time
hours,
Those nightmare hours of loss, of
regret, of longing.

They were entering the Shadowlands.
Even though they had no desire to
tread that way.

And yet He was going ahead of them…

Though the shadows,
He would meet them.

Through the nightmare,
He would reach them.

Through it all,
He would lead them

Beyond

Where night would turn to day.

So who is Jesus?

Jesus is the through and the beyond.

Something to consider

Sometimes life comes crashing down
around you in ways you did not expect
and had not wanted. Even with the
best will in the world, sometimes the
shadows still fall.
In his heart of hearts, Peter did not
want to betray Jesus, and none of
them wanted the things that were to
come. But even as the clouds were
gathering, Jesus was speaking of the
through and the beyond.

For He would lead them through.
There would be a beyond.

Maybe you need to hear today that
even when you feel surrounded by
shadows, God is going ahead of you.
He will lead you through. There will be
a beyond.

Something to pray

My Jesus, sometimes it feels like my
world is crashing around me, and
things I never wanted come my way.
Thank you that you are with me, and
you will lead me through. Thank you
that you beckon me to the beyond,
when you will turn night to day. Amen.

day 67

trusting
deep

"They went to the olive grove called Gethsemane … he
became deeply troubled and distressed. He told them,
'My soul is crushed with grief to the point of death...'
He went on a little farther and fell to the ground. He
prayed that, if it were possible, the awful hour awaiting
him might pass him by. 'Abba, Father,' he cried out,
'everything is possible for you. Please take this cup of
suffering away from me. Yet I want your will to be done,
not mine.'"
[Mark 14v32-42 NLT]

He went to the place of wrestling.

With the heave of heart
Pulled,
In the strain of the fraying.

With the throb of heart
Pressed,
By the weight of the crushing.

He breathed in air dense with sorrow,
And breathed out the ache of surrender.

Counting the cost.

Trusting deep

That Love wins,
Like grace wins,
Like He would win and stand victorious.
And we would forever stand redeemed.

So who is Jesus?

Jesus is the one who trusted deep.

Something to consider

In the garden Jesus prayed a prayer that takes courage to echo: 'Not my will, but yours be done'. Sometimes in our lives, we feel the cost deep. But may we also feel the trust deep.
For Jesus knew the One He was trusting Himself to: The One who is good, the One who loves, the One who is God over all, the One who is working all things together for redemption's sake.

Maybe it was in that garden, in that surrender, that Jesus' victory was secured. For there, He trusted the Father enough to go through with the cross.

May we be bold enough to trust the goodness of God, even as we count the cost. And may we know that there is victory on the other side of surrender. For His love always wins, and in trust deep we are found safe in Him.

Something to pray

Beautiful Jesus, thank you that you counted the cost for me, and that you went through with the cross. I am overwhelmed by your love and forever grateful for your surrender. With deep trust in your love and goodness, I echo the prayer 'Not my will, but your will be done'. Amen.

day 68
costly
moments

"Judas ... arrived with a crowd of men armed with swords and clubs. They had been sent by the leading priests, the teachers of religious law, and the elders. The traitor, Judas, had given them a prearranged signal ... As soon as they arrived, Judas walked up to Jesus. 'Rabbi!' he exclaimed, and gave him the kiss. Then the others grabbed Jesus and arrested him ...
'...these things are happening to fulfil what the Scriptures say about me.'"
[Mark 14v43-52 NLT]

The night was pregnant with the wait
of the years,
And the air seeped through with
promise given.

Hope hinged on each fragile moment,
Each costly moment, each life giving,
death giving moment,
For the time had come.

Now Ushered in on a kiss.

So who is Jesus?

Jesus is the one who owned our
betrayal.

Something to consider

It is hard to grasp what was happening
on that night. There was so much
sorrow held in the moments, and yet
at the same time, the hope of the years
was being realised.

The flesh on flesh.
Breath on breath
Of soft warm trust.

And He was given over to sorrow
pressed down,
Given up to hate pressed in,
Trodden into the dirt
Of soft warm trust

TORN.

So He could own our betrayal.
So we could own Heaven's kiss.

For God Himself was making the way,
God Himself was owning our betrayal,
so that we could receive heaven's kiss.

Whatever the story of your life,
whatever the twists and turns, please
know again that Jesus owned it all so
that you could know heaven's kiss.

Something to pray

Beautiful Jesus, all I can say is thank
you. Thank you that you owned it all so
that I could receive your love, so that I
could receive your acceptance, so that I
could receive heaven's kiss. Amen.

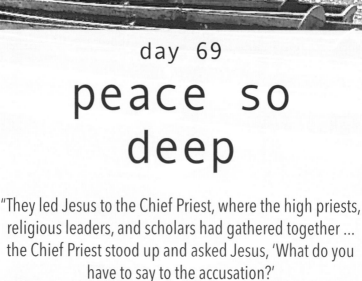

day 69

peace so deep

"They led Jesus to the Chief Priest, where the high priests, religious leaders, and scholars had gathered together ... the Chief Priest stood up and asked Jesus, 'What do you have to say to the accusation?'
Jesus was silent. He said nothing.
The Chief Priest tried again, this time asking, 'Are you the Messiah, the Son of the Blessed?' Jesus said, 'Yes, I am. And you will see the Son of Man seated in the place of power at God's right hand and coming on the clouds of heaven.'
They condemned him, one and all. The sentence: death ... Some of them started spitting at him. They blindfolded his eyes, then hit him, saying, 'Who hit you? Prophesy!' The guards, punching and slapping, took him away."
[Mark 14v53-65 The Message]

And so the tempest began to rain down stored up wrath.

Bellowing thunder loud, striking cruel and hitting fierce
With the hatred of the ages.

The earth trembled at the Holy One dragged on trial,
At the Glorious One pushed through slander.

But He stood in the still and the hush of

Peace
So
Deep.

Knowing that Truth would be seen, as it really is. Grace would be seen, as it really is. He would be seen, as He really is.

Forever the Prince of Peace

So who is Jesus?

Jesus is our Peace.

Something to consider

In the midst of wrongful accusation and grave injustice, Jesus did not try to defend Himself. He trusted God as His eternal defender and His eternal justifier. Therefore in the storm of the situation, He stood with peace so deep.

Standing for truth and standing for justice is important in our broken world. We are called to be a voice for the voiceless and to be bringers of freedom. But how often are we consumed with defending ourselves over things that are really quite minor, and with constantly trying to prove ourselves to others?

Maybe today we could trust ourselves to God, for He is our eternal defender and He is forever our Prince of Peace.

Something to pray

My Jesus, thank you that you are my eternal defender. The knowledge of that brings peace into the temporary storms. I trust you to be the lifter of my head, I trust you to be my Prince of Peace. For now, and for evermore. Amen.

day 70

love runs
deeper

"Meanwhile, Peter was in the courtyard below. One of the servant girls … came by and noticed Peter warming himself at the fire. She looked at him closely and said, 'You were one of those with Jesus of Nazareth.' But Peter denied it … Suddenly, Jesus' words flashed through Peter's mind: 'Before the rooster crows twice, you will deny three times that you even know me.' And he broke down and wept."
[Mark 14v66-72 NLT]

The once upon a fisherlad lingered,
Not wanting to stay, not wanting to leave.

Dreams were being dashed with each beat of time,
Pushing him deep into uncertain hours and a future fragile.

He warmed himself by flames dancing cruel against disappointment,
Wanting to curl up
small,
safe,
held.
It was cold comfort in a world collapsing, in a dream dissolving.
And so he crumbled in the crumbling, and denied the one he loved.

The night seemed colder still and all seemed lost,

For he did not yet know,
Love
Runs
Deeper.

So who is Jesus?

Jesus is the one whose love runs deeper.

Something to consider

For Peter, his world had just collapsed. The one he hoped in, believed in, invested his trust in, and dared his future upon, had been taken. It was not meant to go that way! And in the fear and uncertainty, Peter crumbled.

Sometimes we are like that too.

But that was not the end of Peter's story. After Jesus had risen, He went searching for Peter, restored Peter, and gave him hope for the future.

By the end of the story, Peter knew that Jesus' love ran deeper.

Jesus' love still runs deeper.

Deeper than any mistake, deeper than any regret, deeper than any disappointment. Jesus' love always gives us a hope for the future.

Maybe today you need to curl up small, safe, and held in Jesus' love, knowing His love runs deeper.

Something to pray

My Jesus, thank you that your love runs deeper. I curl up in your love today, knowing that in you I am safe and held. Thank you that you give me hope for the future. I rest in love running deeper. Amen.

day 71

a crowd gathered

"They bound Jesus, led him away, and took him to Pilate, the Roman governor … Now it was the governor's custom each year during the Passover celebration to release one prisoner—anyone the people requested … But at this point the leading priests stirred up the crowd to demand the release of Barabbas instead of Jesus. Pilate asked them, 'Then what should I do with this man you call the king of the Jews?' They shouted back, 'Crucify him!' 'Why?' Pilate demanded. 'What crime has he committed?' But the mob roared even louder, 'Crucify him!'"
[Mark 15v1-15 NLT]

They all gathered.

A mob teeming with mortality,
From pauper to palace.

A mass heaving under the weight of humanity,
From the least to the likely.

A crowd gathered around
One man.

The once upon a promise given.
Light from Light. Truth from Truth. God from God.

And there He stood
Innocent,
Yet owning rejection
For each and every

one.

So who is Jesus?

Jesus is the one who stood for us.

Something to consider

If you look long enough, you can find yourself in the crowd that gathered on that day. There were the religious, the indifferent, the rulers, the commoners, and everyone else in between.

Humanity rejected the Holy, scorned the Rightful, and accused the One from Ancient of Days. He stood for each of us, taking on the weight of us all.

And it makes me fall silent, in awe and gratefulness.

Something to pray

Beautiful Jesus, I cannot take it in… that you would take all the mess, all the dirt, and all the weight of humanity even though you deserved none of it. I fall silent, in awe that you stood for me. Thank you, thank you, thank you. Amen.

day
72
a woven
wreath

"The soldiers took Jesus into the courtyard of the
governor's headquarters … and called out the entire
regiment. They dressed him in a purple robe, and they
wove thorn branches into a crown and put it on his head.
Then they saluted him and taunted, 'Hail! King of the
Jews!' And they struck him on the head with a reed stick,
spit on him, and dropped to their knees in mock worship."
[Mark 15v16-20 NLT]

And behold Him now, The Forever King.
Crowned with such a crown.

Sharp edged. Thistle cruel. Woven in a ring of red.

Encircled in the Twist upon Twine of Thorned earth.

Wrapped in the Snaking Spiral of Ravelled sin.

Pushed through with the Barbed Brokenness
of us all.

And they laughed in the face of God as he wore the wreath,
As he became the one held in the thicket
Of thorned earth.

Spiking in our wounds. Splaying out His grace.

The Forever King.
Crowned
With such a crown.

So who is Jesus?

Jesus is the Forever King.

Something to consider

The Forever King was willingly crowned with our brokenness.

In the garden of Genesis, thorns represented the curse placed on fallen earth. And here, Jesus begins to take the curse for us. All the thorny, broken, painful mess of life and sin, He begins to wear.

On a mountain, God provided a ram to be the sacrifice in place of Abraham's beloved Isaac. Here, Jesus becomes our ram in the thicket – He begins to be the sacrifice for us all.

So behold him now, our Forever King!

Something to pray

My Jesus, you are the Forever King and yet you took my brokenness. You willingly wore it as your own.

Into all the thorny places I welcome your healing, your wholeness, your grace. In my life, I crown you my forever King. Amen.

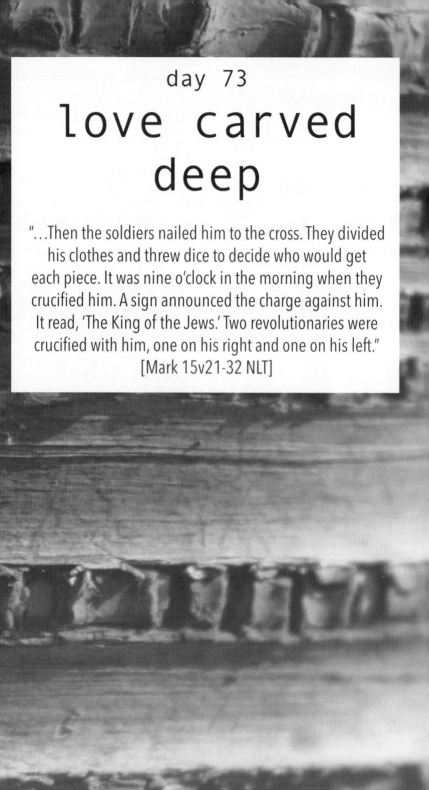

day 73
love carved
deep

"…Then the soldiers nailed him to the cross. They divided his clothes and threw dice to decide who would get each piece. It was nine o'clock in the morning when they crucified him. A sign announced the charge against him. It read, 'The King of the Jews.' Two revolutionaries were crucified with him, one on his right and one on his left."
[Mark 15v21-32 NLT]

See the man upon a tree.
See love carved deep.

Into the forgotten Cries and the Ache of the years,
See love carved deep.

Into steel handed Sorrow and hard nailed Grief,
See love carved deep.

Into the cold edged Cut of Rejected worth
and the Tare of Trust forever Torn.

Into the salted sea of an Earth that Weeps,
And Life so Lost, and Hearts so Dashed upon

All that is Wrong.

See Love Carved Deep.

In His hands. On that tree.
With arms stretched wide in

Love Carved Deep.

So who is Jesus?

Jesus is the one with love carved deep.

Something to consider

On the cross Jesus took it all.

All the loss. All the pain. All the sorrow. All the sickness. All the wrong. All the injustice. All the tears. All the tares. All the punishment that should have been on our shoulders. All the brokenness of everything and everyone.

It was All imprinted in His flesh and etched in His wounds.

Redemption was forever won, in love carved deep.

Something to pray

My Jesus, I cannot take it in. But with a heart full of gratitude and love, I am so thankful for your love carved deep. Amen.

day 74

the shadow
lands

"At noon, darkness fell across the whole land until three
o'clock. Then at three o'clock Jesus called out with a loud voice,
'Eloi, Eloi, lema sabachthani?' which means 'My God, my God,
why have you abandoned me?' … Then Jesus uttered another
loud cry and breathed his last. And the curtain in the sanctuary
of the Temple was torn in two, from top to bottom."
[Mark 15v33-41 NLT]

He gives His last and dark seeps
Into every Sacred space.

Creeping through bone and marrow
Until all is cold.
Until He enters the shadow lands.
The no mans land,
of every man's land,
of earth so torn.

And all is wrenched in this loving.

Until separation Shatters.
And the veil between
Heaven and earth
Rips
Right
Through.

Dark mocks and gathers cold,
But Grace broods Warm
Over us all.

So who is Jesus?

Jesus is the one who shatters
separation.

Something to consider

At the cross, Jesus was paying the
highest price for our freedom. It was
a cost we could never pay in our sin-
covered, dust-covered mess. But
He could in His pure, clean-hearted
righteousness.

God's heart was wrenched in this
loving. For He gave everything to
rescue us out of forever separation
from Him, from forever death.

Jesus paid the innocent blood
price needed for sin's separation
to be broken. He entered death, to
completely destroy the power of that
forever death. And He won back the
rights for us to have open access to
the Father. Making the way for us
to forever have life, in oh-so-warm
relationship with God.

In His death, Jesus shattered the great
separation. Which means that now on
the earth, and for eternal days, we are
never alone for God is with us.

This warm grace is open for any who
will receive it.

Something to pray

My Jesus, thank you that you took
on death itself, to break the power of
forever death. Thank you that you, who
were pure man and Holy God, took the
punishment for all sin's separation,
so that I could have forever life with
you. Thank you that you paid the cost
I could never pay. I trust what you did
on that cross.

Thank you that separation has been
shattered, and now I am never alone.
Thank you that you are with me, now
and for eternity. Amen.

the silent hours

"This all happened on Friday, the day of preparation, the day before the Sabbath ... Joseph bought a long sheet of linen cloth. Then he took Jesus' body down from the cross, wrapped it in the cloth, and laid it in a tomb that had been carved out of the rock. Then he rolled a stone in front of the entrance. Mary Magdalene and Mary the mother of Joseph saw where Jesus' body was laid…"
[Mark 15v42-16v1 NLT]

And the tears fall hard on unyielding ground,
As Shadows Twist in the Torment,
Wrapping cold around every warmth of Fragile Life.

Hope is buried Deep in Death.

And they enter the Silent hours.
Where man mourns,
And God (is closer than we know),
And heaven holds its breath

Waiting

For a Heart beat of Hope

Deep In Life. Deep through Death.

For this is the night silence
Before Redemption's dawn.
And the story is
not
yet
done…

So who is Jesus?

Jesus is the one who brings Redemption's Dawn.

Something to consider

For those who loved Jesus, the end of everything had come. They had seen His death with their own eyes, they had felt it in the ache of their loss, they had known it in the salt of their tears. He was gone.

But the story was not yet done. For God was planning redemption. Even as Jesus was being buried, and even though the silence of Saturday was so real… Sunday was coming.

Sometimes, in our lives, things can seem so dead. Whether that is our dreams, God's promises, or even hope itself. Sometimes we enter those silent hours where we mourn hard. In those times, God is nearer than we know. He is so very close and His heart breaks for us in our sorrow. He never leaves us in those silent hours.

But God is always planning redemption's dawn (in whatever form that may take). And just maybe heaven is holding its breath, for the story is not yet done…

Something to pray

Jesus, you were buried deep in my pain and the brokenness of it all. But the story was not yet done, for your life was about to burst through death.

In the places where I only see an end, where I feel the loss, and where despair comes knocking, I hope again in you. I hold my breath waiting to see what you will do. Please hold me close in these silent hours. Thank you that you can breathe life again into me and into all the buried places. I trust you are always working redemption's dawn. Amen.

day 76

awakening

"Very early on Sunday morning, just at sunrise, they went to the tomb …
the angel said, 'Don't be alarmed. You are looking for Jesus of Nazareth,
who was crucified. He isn't here! He is risen from the dead! Look, this is
where they laid his body. Now go and tell his disciples, including Peter,
that Jesus is going ahead of you to Galilee. You will see him there, just as
he told you before he died.'" [Mark 16v2-8 NLT]

Into the heavy dark,
First glimmers of dawn
Unfurl.

Reaching the edges,
And banishing the shadow hours with
Light.

First tinted pink, then bursting gold, then blazing
With heaven and earth soaked Wonder.

And the world Awakens,
To the unfolding of Grace.
And the women Awaken,
To Love Divine, Love that Wins.

With Life unfolding, with Spirit surrounding,
With Hope kissed warm to life, as He breathes warm to life.

And All things are made New
In the Light of His
Eternal
Dawn

So who is Jesus?

Jesus is God's Eternal Dawn.

Something to consider

Death could not hold Him, the grave could not own Him, and He rose triumphant with Life, clothed in Life, victorious with Life. Making the way for us to have new Life. Now and for eternity.

The women were the first to hear the news of Jesus' resurrection. They didn't fully understand, but they soon would. Where they had once seen only death, new hope and joy would come bursting through, just like with a new dawn.

Jesus' life and light did not stop on that day, they are still blazing out. His life and light still burst through every dark, still make all things new, still bring an eternal dawn. For His Love still wins. His Grace still wins. His sacrifice still wins. And it always will. In Him, it is always a new day.

Let's welcome His resurrection life into all the shadowy places of heart and circumstance, for He loves making all things new. His life is enough to make all the difference and to bring the wonder of His dark banishing, light bringing, hope restoring, new dawn.

Something to pray

Awesome Jesus, you rose forever triumphant in Life. And you made the way for me to have new life in you. Thank you that your life and your light break through any dark. I welcome your life, and am so grateful for the hope of your dawn in me. I am filled with awe and wonder for all you have won for me. Thank you that today is a new day. Amen.

day 77

windswept in wonder

"After Jesus rose from the dead early on Sunday morning, the first person who saw him was Mary Magdalene, the woman from whom he had cast out seven demons. She went to the disciples, who were grieving and weeping, and told them what had happened. But when she told them that Jesus was alive and she had seen him, they didn't believe her." [Mark 16v9-11 NLT]

She was there early in the morning,
Eyes heavy laden with aging sorrow.

The earth was singing dawn,
But she did not hear it, for all had been lost.

Still, she was there. And then…

HIS voice. Shattering every darkened space.
HIS smile. Unraveling death, unraveling grief.
HIS life. Breathing the earth anew.

And she hears it now,
The laughter unfurling,
Awakening the world into Salvation's song.

She grows young again, as light as spirit, windswept in Wonder.

Breathing deep the mystery

God With Us

So who is Jesus?

Jesus is God With Us.

Something to consider

Jesus appeared to Mary. It wasn't just a general gesture, it was personally for her. He met her. He spoke to her. He gave life and hope to her.

Sometimes we can hear the big story of Jesus dying on a cross and rising from the dead, and we know it's so massive that it covers the whole universe. But we can forget that Jesus wants to meet us personally. It's God With Us. The whole story is God With Us. From Genesis to Revelation, it's God With Us.

Not just general, but personal.

He wants to meet with you, speak with you, give life and hope to you. He wants to be with you and walk with you through eternal days.

Something to pray

My Jesus, thank you that you want me. You long to meet with me and walk with me. Thank you that the cross was about God With Us. Now, I can be close to you and you to me. My heart is filled with wonder that you love me so much, that you make redemption's story incredibly personal, so I can be forever found in you. Amen.

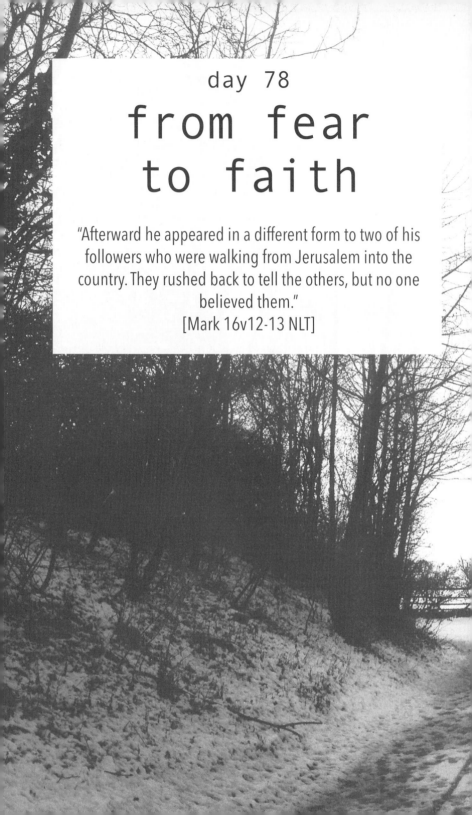

day 78

from fear to faith

"Afterward he appeared in a different form to two of his followers who were walking from Jerusalem into the country. They rushed back to tell the others, but no one believed them."
[Mark 16v12-13 NLT]

The road seemed long.

Pebbled with Questions,
Landscaped in Disappointment,
Riddled right through.

They trod each step,
Feeling uneven ground uncertain
beneath their feet,
Just trying to make sense of it all, just
trying to survive.

And then…
He drew near. Alongside.

This once upon a carpenter.
This one so much more than they had
ever known.

Redefining their path,
Walking them through
Fear
To
Faith.

Where hope surfaced, and Everything
Changed.

So who is Jesus?

Jesus is the one who walks alongside.

Something to consider

These disciples were living the sorrow
and the questions of the story. (And
there must have been many questions
and much sorrow.) But I love it that
Jesus comes alongside them and then
completely redefines their landscape.
Their path was once strewn with loss,
fear, and sadness, but it became a place
of encounter, of hope, and of seeing
more of God than they had ever seen
before. Their lives were completely
changed by Jesus' resurrection, and
their landscape was now defined by a
burning faith in Him.

Sometimes it feels like our path is
just riddled right through. But Jesus
is the one who walks alongside. He
meets us where we are at, loves us,
and then redefines our landscape. He
is always closer than we know, and His
resurrection life changes everything.

May you know that He is walking
alongside you today, and in the
knowledge of who He is – may hope
surface and faith arise.

Something to pray

My Jesus, thank you that you walk
alongside me, even in the questions
and sorrows of the story. Thank you
that you walk me from fear to faith, and
in you everything can change. May my
path become a place of encounter,
where I see you more and know you
more. May hope arise in me and faith
burn bright, as I gaze upon you. Amen.

day 79

the beginning and the end

"Still later, as the Eleven were eating supper, he appeared and took them to task most severely for their stubborn unbelief, refusing to believe those who had seen him raised up."
[Mark 16v14 The Message]

And now they see.

The once upon a carpenter,
The one who holds
The beginning
and
The end.

And all the mixed up letters find their place,
As the story comes together in Him.

And the once upon a fisherlads are wide-eyed,
At the grandeur of God displayed
In Scarred Hands
And a Pierced Side.

For His Grace wins,
His Love wins,
His Life wins.

And now they see their Lord.

The Beginning
and
The End.

So who is Jesus?

Jesus is The Beginning and The End.

Something to consider

This was the moment where everything changed for the disciples, including Peter, for they saw Jesus with their own eyes. All the confusion and all the sorrow of the last days, dissolved with what they now beheld. For the one they had hoped was the Messiah, was truly the Messiah.

Jesus was alive, God was with them and had chosen them.

The story was always in God's hands, and it all came together in Jesus.

It still is and does, today.

Something to pray

My Jesus, thank you that you bear the scars of love that won for me, of grace that won for me, of life that won for me. I am in awe of you, beautiful one. Thank you that all the story comes together in you. Thank you that you are always The Beginning and The End. Amen.

day
80
good news imprinted

"Then he said, 'Go into the world. Go everywhere and announce the Message of God's good news to one and all. Whoever believes and is baptized is saved; whoever refuses to believe is damned. These are some of the signs that will accompany believers: They will throw out demons in my name, they will speak in new tongues, they will take snakes in their hands, they will drink poison and not be hurt, they will lay hands on the sick and make them well.'"
[Mark 16v15-18 The Message]

And now the message is rolled out wide.

And it's good news
For the weary, and the broken, and the ones covered in the dust of the earth.
It's good news
For the tired, and the tied up, and the ones caught in the highs and the lows.
It's good news
For the near, and the dear, and the ones far from Home.

This good news inscribed on awakened hearts,

Each letter of Grace emblazoned in flesh,
Each word of Hope imprinted on the pulse,

Etched in the marrow of our being,
Impressed deep into our breathing,
Carrying Life to the core.

Publishing wide the wonder,
Spreading wide the welcome,

Our
God
Will
Save.

So who is Jesus?

Jesus is the good news.

Something to consider

God's story was always about redemption. It wasn't just for the disciples gathered way back then, it was always meant for the ends of the earth, for all of time. And His redemption, this good news, is rolled out in glorious life, power, and grace, for whoever will believe and receive.

No exclusions. No elitism. No favoritism. It is for Whoever.

Which means it is wide enough to cover you and me.

This really is good news!

Something to pray

My Jesus, thank you for this good news. Thank you for your saving grace, which is wide enough to cover us all. Thank you that I can never earn or deserve such a gift, but you have given it freely to me at your own personal cost. I believe. I receive. I am so grateful that I am forever found in your good news. May your life be so imprinted in me that it spreads out to others, so that they may find your welcome in this everlasting good news. Amen.

day
81

written in

"Then the Master Jesus, after briefing them, was taken up to heaven, and he sat down beside God in the place of honor. And the disciples went everywhere preaching, the Master working right with them, validating the Message with indisputable evidence."
[Mark 16v19-20 The Message]

So with battle fought and battle won, the unlikely are written in and commissioned with The Story...

His Story, which is Redemption's Story, which is now Their Story...

Of how the rightful King
Paid in blood,
To establish again
Redemption's reign.

And the earthen ones
Born from the dust,
Can be clothed in grace
For forever days.

How He wears the scars
Of love carved deep,
How he wears the crown
Of it All Complete.

And Redemption's tale
Unfurls and unfolds,
Written in Spirit
Both tender and bold.

So behold Him now
The Eternal Son,

God With Us,

The Glorious One.

So who is Jesus?

Jesus is the Glorious One.

Something to consider

When Jesus sat down in the place of honour at God's right hand, it showed it was all done. The work of the cross was complete, the debt was paid, the victory assured. He is forever the Eternal Son, the Glorious One who made the way for us to have peace with God.

And it was a new beginning of living out God's story on the earth for the disciples. For Jesus would be with them, be in them, and be working through them by His Spirit.

Their lives were now part of God's unfolding story. They were forever written in.

Just as our lives are now part of His unfolding story. We are forever written in.

Something to pray

Beautiful Jesus, you are the Glorious One. You are forever seated in the place of honour, You deserve all praise and all glory. You have my trust, my devotion, and my adoration. I am so grateful for your love and your grace.

Thank you that you have written me into your story of redemption. Thank you that you are forever with me. Thank you that you want to work in me, and through me, and with me, so others may find their place in your glorious, wonderful, grace-filled story. Amen.

journey's end

So, I began these musings in a red notebook.

They were seeded small, just in a tiny thought and easily passed by. But there was a hunger within me to know Him more, and so I began a journey through journals, typewriter ink, and computer pages. A journey deeper into Him. A journey which turned into these 'Musings Through Mark'. A journey I have absolutely loved.

Landscapes changed as the path unfolded, and I am forever changed through the process.

I had no idea how these reflections would be written, and felt completely daunted by the task. However, God has surprised me each and every day, because He is like that! And even though these entries are just some thoughts and ramblings, and these photographs just an attempt to see moments, it makes me wonder what He is longing to do with us, through us, and in us, if we make room.

For His story is always unfolding, from glory to glory.

Thank you so much for journeying with me.

I really pray these musings have been good for the heart. I really pray we might all know Him more, as we find ourselves written into His great story of grace.

And … as we discover ourselves within His story, may we

Write it glorious
With His life

Write it glorious
With His grace

Write it glorious
With His love

For God is with us.

Much Love
Sarah

Space to Dream...

About the Author

Sarah has loved the story of things ever since childhood days, when the neighbourhood would gather in their front room to see Christmas plays performed.

The love of words continued and Sarah became a performance storyteller and writer with Footprints Theatre Trust. After her years at Footprints, Sarah spent seasons in the sunshine of Australia. Through her time there she continued to write short film scripts and story scripts for use in her local context, where she was part of an incredible creative team in a wonderful church family.

She now lives and works as a writer in London and continues to fall more in love with Jesus, the great Storyteller. Sarah likes a good cup of tea, a good story, and a good crisp autumn day.

Deepest thanks to...

My heart friends and mentors who have walked the journey with me. You are all part of the story so far and I am forever grateful. xxx

Also my heartfelt thanks to Malcolm Down (publisher), Tim Pettingale (designer), Jan Moys (proof reader) and Folaju Oyegbesan (for the author photo).